PRAISE FOR

BETTER TOGETHER

"I am delighted to see *Better Together* by Robert J. Matz and John Mark Yeats. The two authors serve as cherished colleagues at Midwestern Seminary, and the book they have written ought to be must-reading for all Southern Baptists. Central to God's work through Southern Baptists over the past several generations has been the ingenuity and generosity channeled by the Cooperative Program. Yet, what Southern Baptists have certainly benefitted from is in danger of being lost. Yeats and Matz make a compelling case why every congregation should give sacrificially through the Cooperative Program and, as they do, how the world can more effectively be reached for Christ."
–Jason K. Allen, Ph.D., President, Midwestern Baptist Theological Seminary

"Yeats and Matz have produced something that should resonate with multiple generations of committed Southern Baptists. His understanding of history and how Southern Baptists work together have helped him develop a resource which can be used for decades to come. *Better Together* speaks to the sense of togetherness Southern Baptists can experience

when they voluntarily and sacrificially give through the Cooperative Program. No other denomination has been so blessed with a God-given tool to impact the world as the people called Southern Baptists. Better Together reveal the genesis and the genius of that story. I recommend to my Southern Baptist family as guide for better understanding the eternal impact of giving through the Cooperative Program."
– Rick Lance, Executive Director, Alabama Baptist Convention

"Southern Baptists cooperate together not just because it's effective, but because it's biblical. I am thoroughly convinced that partnership for the advancement of the gospel is among the New Testament's most significant themes, and I love partnering with others to see the gospel known among the nations. I'm thankful that Yeats and Matz have worked together to provide a compelling argument about the importance of our cooperation. This is a strong and helpful work that can serve to better advance God's redemptive purposes."
– Micah Fries, Senior Pastor, Brainerd Baptist Church, Chattanooga, TN

"I encourage you to read *Better Together*. The Cooperative Program is more than a plan; it is about people. John Mark and Robert highlight the Christ-honoring aspects of the Southern Baptist giving plan. He reminds us we are in gospel work together."
– Jim Richards, Executive Director, Southern Baptist Convention of Texas

"I love my family – my wife, our children, their spouses and our grandchildren. I cannot imagine life without them. I also love my faith family – the Southern Baptist Convention (SBC). I've been part of the SBC all my life. Like family, I don't always agree with everything Southern Baptists do. But I still love and believe in the SBC. Our missionaries, colleges, seminaries, and other entities are financially supported by a vehicle called the Cooperative Program (CP). Regardless of size, any church can be part of the SBC's worldwide work by giving to the CP. In their new book, *Better Together: You, Your Church, and the Cooperative Program*, Robert J. Matz and John M. Yeats, both veteran "SBCers", provide a wonderful resource emphasizing that all SBC churches can do more if we work cooperatively rather than independently. I'm grateful for the authors, whom I know and love, and I enthusiastically recommend this insightful and valuable resource."
– Steve Gaines, PhD, Senior Pastor, Bellevue Baptist Church, Memphis, TN

"This will be a valuable resource for churches to use to help equip their people. The study questions provide a good starting point for next steps. I would highly recommend churches using this book as a tool for membership classes or any other venue where they want to help their people see their church as the mission sending agent that God has called them to be."
– Charles Campbell, Manager, Send Network Planter Training

"The best Southern Baptist primer on the Cooperative Program. It is simple and well written and should be a part of every new member class in the local church and a part of every church plant."
– Bob Mills, Executive Director, Kansas-Nebraska State Convention

"A Great work! This is very current and appropriate resource for the typical church member."
– Hance Dilbeck, Executive Director, Baptist General Convention of Oklahoma

"*Better Together* is a much-needed, accurate, simple resource for participants in Southern Baptist churches. It is also a superb primer for those who are brand new to a local Southern Baptist church or for church leaders in evangelical congregations wondering who Southern Baptists are. The key to the success of cooperative missions and ministries has always been the pastor educating the people he shepherds with the truth about our comprehensive work. I can envision a pastor leading his congregation through a 7-week study of *Better Together* to equip them with understanding about why his local church the biblical basis and practical engagement with the Cooperative Program."
– John L. Yeats, Executive Director of the Missouri Baptist Convention and Recording Secretary of the Southern Baptist Convention

"In a world that is increasingly divided and fragmented, provides a much-needed reminder of the power of cooperation for advancing the Great Commission. Matz and Yeats do a masterful job of telling the story of how the Gospel is spread more rapidly and effectively as Southern Baptists work together, rather than in isolation, to get the Gospel to the ends of the earth."
– Gary Hollingsworth, Executive Director of the South Carolina Baptist Convention

"*Better Together* explains the simple genius of the Cooperative Program. As a life-long Baptist, I assumed I knew the Cooperative Program backwards and forwards, but I learned a great deal from this resource. I plan to pass out *Better Together* to new members of the church I pastor so they can learn where our CP dollars go and the incredible impact we have when Southern Baptists work together. We truly are better together."
– Mark Spence, Pastor, Mississippi Avenue Baptist Church, Colorado

"What is the best way for your church to fulfill the Great Commission? While some prefer to work alone in fulfilling our Lord's missionary command, Yeats and Matz advocate the Southern Baptist experience with the Cooperative Program. In seven interesting, informative, and compelling chapters, they show why and how the churches work 'better together' to bring the gospel into the world. This short book is

biblical, evangelical, and practical, and it comes with my hearty recommendation."
– Malcolm Yarnell, Research Professor of Systematic Theology, Southwestern Baptist Theological Seminary, Fort Worth, Texas

"*Better Together* is the best work I have encountered that couples an overview of the Cooperative Program with a biblical study of the local church's role in Great Commission work. A pastor could easily implement it as a short study of how the local church functions in mission, utilize it in helping new members understand the church's connection to the Southern Baptist Convention, or use it to ensure that those in key leadership positions understand the role of the church's participation in the Cooperative Program."
– Scott Gilbert, Frederick Boulevard Baptist Church, Missouri

"There is no doubt that the Cooperative Program has proven to be the most effective and efficient way to fund missionaries across North America and around the world. Yet sometimes churches lose the personal touch with the missionaries they support. *Better Together* brings the Cooperative Program to life, as each chapter puts a new face on the ministries it supports. Not only will readers come to a fuller understand of how the Cooperative Program works, they will also encounter real life stories of people personally impacted by it."
– Matthew Marrs, NAMB Send Network Regional Director

"When I reflect on the Cooperative Program, I can't help but think of the words used as the title, 'better together.' We better the kingdom, together. We better reach the lost, together. We better invest locally, regionally, nationally, and globally, together. As Southern Baptists, we only become better, together. I wholeheartedly endorse this great primer on the Cooperative Program!"
– Michael Criner, Pastor, First Baptist Church Bellville, Texas

"Good summation of our Southern Baptist work—why we do it and how we do it."
– David Hankins, Executive Director, Louisiana Baptist Convention

BETTER TOGETHER

YOU, YOUR CHURCH, AND THE COOPERATIVE PROGRAM

Robert J. Matz
John M. Yeats

Better Together: You, Your Church, and
the Cooperative Program

© 2019 by Robert J. Matz and John M. Yeats
All rights reserved.

ISBN: 978-1-948022-10-1

Rainer Publishing
www.RainerPublishing.com
Spring Hill, TN

Printed in the United States of America

To my parents, Will and Carol, who taught me to love Southern Baptist churches and our collective work.
-Robert

To my parents and the generations of faithful Southern Baptists who continue to engage the world with the gospel through Cooperative Program
-John Mark

CONTENTS

FOREWORD

I f I have learned one thing about the Cooperative Program (and I am always learning new things about it), it is that no matter how well it has performed in the past, no matter how much it has produced, no matter how prolific, pertinent, or clear the instruction about it is, and no matter how many times examples about it and pleas to examine and test it are given, there will always be an audience who has never heard any of those things, and thousands more whose trust in CP needs to be reinforced by being reminded of all those things. Of course, the same things are true about understanding how our Southern Baptist Convention works.

Additionally, I am absolutely convinced that if those introductions and reminders ceased, even for as short a time as two or three years, appreciation for our Convention structure and its Cooperative Program would plummet, and that would be a tragedy.

This potential for a "dark ages" in ministry funding, or in trust of our processes, is reason enough to applaud another new work that lifts those things up to inspection and appreciation. But as I was reading through *Better Together* for the first time, I realized that it presents our SBC structure and our Cooperative Program through a lens that makes an epiphany about them more possible and a commitment to them more probable. For that reason, I do not consider *Better Together* "just another new work" promoting preferred paradigms. It is much better than that. It explains how our structure and ministry-funding mechanism are drawn from biblical models. Said another way, this book, in a very basic and easy-to-understand way, helps people understand that Southern Baptists do what we do in the way we do it because we believe we are following God's instruction manual—His Word—the Bible.

The books title sums it up nicely in just two words—*better together*. I offer the following story as an illustration of why I think the title is perfect.

Most everyone knows what a mainspring is. It is also pretty common knowledge that every analog watch needs at least two hands, a watch face, a crystal, etc. Maybe a slightly smaller crowd understands the functions of jewels in the internal workings of an older, non-electronic time piece. An even fewer number of folks would recognize other small parts required to make a wind-up watch operational, such as a stem, a balance wheel, a regulator or an escape.

One day a watchmaker who owned and ran a sizeable shop found himself in need of a new bench worker, so he posted an ad which produced results, generating three applicants. He invited them all to his place of business at the same time for initial interviews, after which he showed them all around the shop, introducing them to the other workers, familiarizing them with the layout of the place and the division of work, and pointing out the various timepieces that were there for repair or cleaning.

As the applicants became more comfortable with their guide and each other, the conversation between flowed freely and easily and the stiffness of formality diminished. Questions were posed and answered, comments were offered, and observations were made, all of which the watchmaker had hoped would happen.

At one unoccupied bench there was a pile of watch parts (such as I described above) gathered together in the middle of the work surface. The first applicant asked, "What's that?" The second applicant, smiling and thinking he was about to obtain an upper hand, proudly proclaimed "That is an old, lever-set, Seth Thomas pocket watch."

After the tour, on their way out, the owner pulled the third applicant aside and asked why he was not the one to answer the question the first applicant had asked about the pile of parts. The third applicant said, "I did not want to be rude or appear to be argumentative. I knew the parts appeared to be for an 1892 Seth Thomas triple-lid, but I could not tell if they were all there. For that reason, I did not consider them to really be a watch. The parts are not a watch until they are all there, are all put together properly, and are all operating as they are meant to."

The watchmaker said "You are hired."

In that sense, we Southern Baptists are truly *Better Together*.

It is my prayer that your reading of this book will help you see and appreciate not only the intent of our Convention and each of its component parts, nor even the elegance of their individual design and functionality, but to see our structure and funding plan and the churches and people involved in those things (*you*)—all of those parts *together*—as a fitting and suitable way to do all the Lord has asked us to do as we follow His will.

D. August Boto
Interim President
Executive Committee of the SBC
July 2018

INTRODUCTION

You can make a difference.
I know you've been told that all of your life, but what if it were true?

What if I told you that there is a group of Christians who work together to share the gospel with millions of people all over the world every year? What if I told you that this group leads nearly 500,000 people to Christ annually? What if I told you this same group starts over 6,000 churches outside the United States and nearly 1,000 churches in the United States each year?

What if I told you that these people are changing the world not only by sharing their faith in Christ but also by living it out? What if I told you that this group acts as one the nation's largest disaster-relief providers, serving over two million meals to disaster victims each year and volunteering 100,000 work days toward rebuilding projects?

What if I told you this group passionately connected African-American and Caucasian church leaders to fight racial injustice and animosity? What if I told you that they fund ministries all over the country to protect the lives of the unborn? What if, because they value life from its first to final moments, they also oversaw facilities for abandoned children and cared for those entering their twilight years without adequate resources?

These people are Southern Baptists. Our churches may vary in size and style, but we are fiercely committed to one thing: sharing the hope of Jesus Christ around the world.

This is where you enter the picture.

Each church in the Southern Baptist Convention comprises people just like you. We are farmers and teachers, students and retirees, business people and homemakers. We come from all walks of life, and we all love Jesus and want people to experience the life-giving truth of the gospel. We know this truth: God did not save us to leave us on our own.

We are better together.

Isn't that incredible? We come together weekly in our churches for worship. We cooperate together to serve our communities directly through specialized ministries. We know that we can do so much more together as a church than any one person could ever do.

We are better together.

This same principle applies to our churches as well. Our congregations are independent, but we strategically band together to do more than any single congregation ever could.

Support Missionaries? You bet.

Train pastors and leaders? Of course.

Pool resources to plant churches? Without a doubt!

Send people to help those in need? YES!

Share Jesus with a lost world? Is there even a question here? That's the whole point!

Baptists have always held the idea of cooperating together as a value. It's part of our DNA. That's why, in 1925, Baptists overwhelmingly approved the genius of what became known as the Cooperative Program. Instead of different organizations vying for the attention of each local congregation, we decided we could maximize our impact for the Kingdom of God by sharing together in one great, comprehensive work.

Participation was voluntary, but churches quickly caught on to the power of working together. Through this cooperative venture Southern Baptists created the largest Protestant missionary sending force in the world. More missionaries. More pastors trained. More churches started. More people coming to know Jesus.

It was a win on all sides, and it still is.

And it's why this book is important. This study is about the congregations and people who make up these churches and how they are working together to change the world. You and your church can change the world with them if you dare.

HOW CHURCHES ARE CHANGING THE WORLD

Our story starts exactly where it should—the local church. We will discover how all these unique and separate churches can come together through a shared commitment to the gospel of Jesus Christ and the Word of God. As churches rally around this common belief, we lay the foundation for engaging the world.

From our local churches Baptists engage their local and regional communities. We will uncover the story of how Baptist churches are committed to changing their homes, cities, and states through the work of local associations and state conventions in chapter 2. Through this often-overlooked side of ministry, churches change their regions and minister to those in greatest need.

Not only are these churches committed to their local mission fields, they are also committed to bringing the Gospel message to their nation. Chapter 3 tells of the work of the North American Mission Board and how this mission entity partners with churches to evangelize, plant new churches, and provide disaster relief throughout North America.

The centerpiece of the Cooperative Program is the International Mission Board. For over 170 years Southern Baptists have committed to bringing the gospel message to every nation, every tribe, and every people. The International Mission Board empowers local churches to do just that. As we'll discover in chapter 4, through their work millions become Christ-followers and human needs are met all over the globe.

The demands of the gospel change the world and even reshape our society. Chapter 5 explains how the Ethics and Religious Liberty Commission partners with churches to further racial reconciliation and to work in our society to protect lives, marriages, and families. We will also explore why Baptists are so passionately committed to religious liberty.

Chapter 6 turns to examine how churches come together to train the next generation of leaders through education. Investing in our colleges and seminaries allows for a biblical worldview to permeate the lives of the next generation of church leaders as we seek to engage our culture.

With over 15 million Southern Baptists placing their trust in the Cooperative Program, wise leadership, transparency and accountability are essential. The final chapter explains the leadership structures for the Cooperative Program and how those structures are answerable to each church and its individual members.

You and your church are not alone.

Together we can do more for the kingdom by cooperating as Southern Baptists.

Together we can make a difference.

CHAPTER ONE:

HOW YOUR CHURCH CAN CHANGE THE WORLD

One hundred people stood with a long rope slack in their hands. In front of them a simple line painted on the black runway marked the finish line. Behind them, attached to the rope, stood a glistening 747-400 jumbo jet.

The goal was simple: the team of one hundred people needed to pull the 463,000-pound plane across the finish line one hundred yards away.

The horn sounded.

They pulled.

They strained.

The plane started to move.

The crowd went nuts. Empowered by the cheering, the team pressed on harder toward their goal. Placing one foot deliberately in front of the other in a synchronized rhythm, the team advanced to the finish line. Every pull was a battle, yet together they were doing the impossible!

As the plane crossed the finish line, the team collapsed into an exhausted heap on the ground, and the crowd began to cheer even louder! They had done it! They set the world record for the heaviest aircraft pulled over one hundred yards by a team.

TEAMWORK MAKES THE DIFFERENCE

In congregations across America, people gather on Sunday to worship God together. As they gather, they sing songs, participate in learning the Scriptures, and encourage one another. Each of these services looks and feels different, yet each strives to be consistent with the scriptural understanding of a congregation because we are the body of Christ.

The "church as the Body of Christ" is an interesting scriptural picture. We are the visible manifestation of Christ on earth. We are the hands and feet to get the work done. Together, church members represent the beauty and diversity of the body of Christ to a lost and dying world.

The term "church" is translated from the Greek term *ekklesia*, which means "a gathered people." Because each congregation is an intentional gathering of a wide variety of people, each church looks and feels different from the next. It's part of God's design. Not only does gathering together matter, it changes us as individuals.

There's an inherent appeal here. Why do these people who claim the name of Jesus gather every Sunday? Why do they sing songs and listen to sermons? Why does there seem to be no socioeconomic stratification? Why do their families look different than the rest of the world?

Everywhere else in our world, people gather for different, temporal reasons. They gather to support their favorite sports teams or to rally for political parties. They pay to be a part of country clubs or formal organizations.

It's not the gathering that's different. It's the *reason* for the gathering that shifts the entire picture. That reason is eternal and spiritual.

The *reason* for our gathering is to celebrate our risen Savior Jesus Christ. As a community of faith, we are "keeping our eyes on Jesus, the source and perfecter of our faith" (Heb 12:2).[1]

This should be natural for us. In Colossians 1:18 the Apostle Paul writes a sweeping hymn of praise about Jesus. We are told, "He is also the head of the body, the church."[2]

Jesus is the one who leads and is the head of everything in our congregation.

But let's be honest. This trips a lot of people up. Our focus is often on the pastor or other church leadership roles, not on Jesus.

Here's the thing—Baptists have always been clear about articulating this core principle: The **church is God's plan and Jesus is the head of the church**.

> As the doorbell rang Lisa could hardly hold back the tears. Another church member stood at her door with a special gift—a casserole. Ever since her diagnosis with a brain tumor a year ago, the church stepped up care for her family in ways she couldn't measure.
>
> To be honest, Lisa struggled with the outpouring of love through these fellow church members. She felt guilty. Over the past couple of years, baseball and kids had kept them out of Bible study and church attendance. Yet the church still called and invited. Teachers sent notes to the kids in the mail. The church still called and checked in on them despite the self-imposed distance.
>
> The moment the church heard about her diagnosis, they showered Lisa and her family with love. Even though Lisa and her family tried to ignore their church family, during this moment of crisis the church entered a new level of ministry to show their love. Pastors showed up to the hospital and walked with their family through the pain of chemo and treatment. Small group leaders prayed and helped with transporting Lisa's kids to games and school events.
>
> Never before had Lisa seen the power of the local congregation. She began to wonder, "How do people without Jesus and a local church make it?"

LET'S GET PERSONAL

Christianity begins and ends with Jesus.

At some point each of us heard the clear communication of the gospel—the good news—of Jesus. We connected to his miraculous birth; his perfect, sinless life; and his death, burial, and resurrection. We trusted that only through Christ could we have the forgiveness of sin. We knew that without Jesus we were destined to eternal separation from God.

When we trusted Jesus as Savior, God did something amazing in our lives.

We became new. He changed us from the inside out. He gave us his Spirit who works inside of us to make us more like Jesus. Suddenly, God's Word mattered more than it ever did before. We saw true, spiritual growth in our personal lives as we embraced the working of the gospel in our life.

Even more dynamically, God changed our status. Those who once were far off and alienated were brought near. God adopted us spiritually and made us part of his family. Fellow believers became brothers and sisters. We connect with Christians on a global scale that transcends geographical boundaries because the one aspect that now marks our lives is Jesus.

But this can be a hard concept. Sure, we get the idea of personal salvation, but is it really that important that we understand the idea of a family of faith and entrance into a community?

I met Max during an evangelistic outreach.

"I worship God every week," he stated. "Every Sunday I get in my truck, head to the lake, and fish. In the quiet of that time, I think of the Man Upstairs and worship him there. I don't need a church."

Max passionately believed that the best way for him to worship God was alone. He thought Jesus was a good teacher and that many people could be helped by a church. It just wasn't for him. He typified what Dan Kimball called, "loving Jesus, but not the church."[3]

Spend time with those disconnected from the community of faith and you will hear the myriad of excuses of why church isn't for them.

People aren't loving.

They're all hypocrites.

They fight all the time.

I don't like the music.

The staff don't love the people.

They demand too much from people.

The list goes on and on.

But the Bible makes it clear that God's best for you and for me is to immerse ourselves in the community of faith. Consider the fifty-nine "one anothers" in the New Testament, such "love one another" (I Thess. 4:9), "Encourage one another" (Hebrews 10:25), and "Pray for one another" (James 5:16). None of these things can be done very well alone.

To be even more pointed, we are hardwired for community. Even the most introverted person in your congregation needs the family of God to grow and mature. Notice the dynamism of the church in the book of Acts. People in the church worshiped together in settings both large and small. Christians "ate together from house to house." (Acts 2:46) They sent missionaries like Paul and Silas out in teams to reach the lost together. Churches in some cities even gave money to help congregations in other regions that were struggling.

Being alone will only get you so far.

Together, as a body of believers—the church—we accomplish so much more because it is part of the design of God.

THE IDEA OF CHURCH

Baptists like to remind people that the church is not a place; it's a people. Buildings are nice, but they aren't the church. We technically don't "go" to church because we *are* the church.

This changes the way we think and talk about congregations and how we worship. Think with me for a second.

If the church is the body of Christ, if Jesus is the head of the church, *and* if the church is part of God's design, we should expect some amazing things to happen in our congregations.

In Ephesians, the Apostle Paul encouraged the church to look at this idea. He starts by reminding the congregation of their salvation in Christ. Go read the first two chapters. Both are masterful portrayals of the salvation God brings though Jesus. There's no escaping how great our salvation truly is.

Every time our church baptizes someone, the congregation gets to hear the story of how that person came to faith in Christ. It never ceases to amaze any of us of how far the love of God goes to reach even the most wayward of souls with the gospel. As the person finishes sharing, they are placed under the water, declaring their new allegiance to Christ as Lord.

If that weren't enough, Paul turns the reader's focus to how God does something unexpected. God is bringing people from all walks of life and from every corner of the globe into the family of God. This blows Paul away. It's all too much. How could

31

it be that the God of creation would create a new entity—the church-for the purpose of bringing even more glory to God?

Paul helps us see this plan unfold more explicitly. He states:

> This is so God's multi-faceted wisdom may now be made known through the church to the rulers and authorities in the heavens. This is according to his eternal purpose accomplished in Christ Jesus our Lord. (Eph 3:10–11)

God's plan all along was to gather a people who don't look like each other, sound like each other, or come from the same side of the tracks as each other. But he brings them into the same family through the work of Jesus. This, Paul says, is God's *wisdom*. It is his plan. It's been God's plan since before time began (v. 11). Followers of Jesus become part of the plan as they work and worship in the community of faith.

That's why church matters. It's God's design. When we gather together with other believers and center on the person and work of Jesus Christ, we celebrate God's eternal wisdom. But our gathering does something else. Our gathering boldly proclaims the wisdom of God to a lost world: " . . . so that God's multi-faceted wisdom may now be *made known through the church*" (v. 10, emphasis added). In being the church, our congregations visibly make known the wisdom of God's salvation through Jesus Christ.

That's amazing!

You may not feel like gathering on a Sunday with other believers, but the Word of God helps us understand that in our times together we are proclaiming the gospel to the lost. It's more than just a meeting time with a few songs, readings of Scripture, and a sermon. It's a powerful moment that God uses to illustrate the very essence of the gospel!

The final part of verse 10 points to something we should never miss: our gathering proclaims the gospel "to rulers and authorities in the heavens." That means our time together on Sundays or those times we gather to do the work of ministry are boldly declaring to all of creation that Jesus is Lord! Every demon, every angel, every corner of creation reverberates with the sound of praise from the people of God pointing to Jesus as Lord.

Just as God designed.

PULLING IN THE SAME DIRECTION

Gathering raises the stakes. Our identity as the people of God under the lordship of Jesus Christ matters in the grand scheme of God's design.

This is why we must pay attention to being effective congregations working together for the sake of the gospel. Time is short and the stakes are high as we seek to accomplish his work. So we push forward *together.*

Much like the team that pulled the jet, the members of a congregation need to be pulling in the same direction. There must be an agreed-upon foundation

33

so they can work in unity. This is often why effective churches have a clearly articulated faith statement. While believers may have a variety of opinions about different things, effective churches possess a clearly defined statement that outlines precisely what they believe.

Once individuals in a congregation understand their shared values, they can walk together in harmony and fully represent Jesus to a lost world. When the watching world asks, we can boldly state, "This we believe."

This same principle applies when multiple churches work together to accomplish broader goals. We need shared values that enable us to agree on the essential matters. This is why Baptists historically held to confessions of faith. Not only did these become foundational for understanding what an individual congregation believed, but they also allowed congregations to multiply their work by partnering with congregations of like faith and practice to accomplish the broader work of the ministry.

In the chapters that follow, we will be diving into ideas about how multiple congregations can accomplish amazing things if they work together. If done well, your church can make a difference all the way to the ends of the earth.

Of course, that all starts right in your own backyard. Let's find out how in the next chapter as we explore how your church can change your state.

KEY QUESTIONS:

1. Why shouldn't we think about the church as a destination?

2. Why does gathering in the local church matter? Why shouldn't we just worship God on our own?

3. What's at stake in the local church gathering?

4. Based on Ephesians 3:10, what happens when the church comes together?

5. Why should the members of a congregation all pull in the same direction?

CHAPTER TWO:

HOW YOUR CHURCH CAN CHANGE YOUR REGION

I s there anything better than Blue Bell ice cream on a hot summer day?

If you live in Texas or the surrounding states, you know exactly what I'm talking about. Fresh cream blended with all kinds of goodies for the best ice cream around!

Blue Bell's commitment to freshness meant that for many years, the only place you could get a scoop of their ice cream was to make a quick trip to the Lone Star State. Talk to any Texan who no longer resides within the state and Blue Bell is one of the things they miss the most. It is by far a regional favorite.

Every state seems to have their favorites. In Illinois it's Oberweis. In Missouri it's Central Dairy. Visit Ohio and you better grab a cone of Jeni's. These regional dairy farms combine the best of the fresh farm produce of the region into a favorite for anyone to who lives in that area.

REACHING OUR REGION

Food is one of the unique things that defines our experiences in a given region. It also becomes part of how we understand our unique heritage. From state university sports rivalries to the musical genres we embrace, we recognize the special distinctions that set each place apart while also providing a framework for flourishing.

State conventions in the Southern Baptist Convention serve as the regional leaders helping churches connect with their home towns, their broader communities, and the needs of their regions. Their goal is simple—serve the churches in our region to accomplish more together for the sake of the gospel.

The SBC is known for its fierce commitment to the priority of the local church. Each congregation recognizes Jesus as the head of the church and the members as the body who accomplish the work of ministry. It's an incredible, freeing way to see the people of God rise up and fulfill their calling!

While each church ministers to the surrounding community, there are often jobs that are too large for one congregation to take on alone. We can do more together, whether it is helping fund a biblically grounded Baptist university, effective senior citizen care, or work with children who need foster care or adoption, these ministries can't happen on their own. Churches working together bring solutions that make a difference for each region to reach out to others.

As churches aim to make a difference, state conventions in the SBC help churches engage the region more strategically. The specific needs in St. Louis are different than the specific needs of congregations in Birmingham. Since they know their region best, state convention leaders serve as missionaries to the states and regions they serve.

THINK LIKE A MISSIONARY

When we send missionaries to work in areas around the globe, each trained individual begins a very important task—figuring out how to communicate the truth of the gospel in the region where they are deployed. They learn about the culture, study the language, and seek out how to best advance the gospel in that specific context. As their work progresses, they set out to train new Christians and deepen them in the faith so the local believers can eventually take over the mission work in their country.

Why?

Because if you are "from there," you can reach more of the people "from there."

Who knows your state best? Who knows your city or town best? The people who live there already. That's you! That's your church!

If we begin to think like missionaries, our congregations become the hub of activity for gospel advance

---

Ministry Spotlight: Baptist Disaster Relief

In April of 2017, no one expected the deluge of rain and storms that pummeled southern Missouri. As the rivers rose, the rain never seemed to stop. Eventually the water levels peaked around forty feet above flood stage. Whole houses disappeared, businesses were destroyed, and lives altered.

Local churches in Missouri jumped into action. They mobilized volunteers to work with their regional disaster relief teams to start the clean-up process by helping restore the area. They served meals and provided clean showers and laundry facilities. Even more critical—they shared the hope of Jesus with people who lost everything.

For over fifty years disaster relief has served as a key point for state conventions to make a difference in their own region and beyond. When our network of regional disaster relief organizations is mobilized together through the North American Mission Board, Southern Baptist Disaster Relief is now the third largest relief organization in the United States, with over 70,000 trained volunteers.

Even better, the effort and work of Baptist Disaster Relief is supported financially through the gifts of churches through the Cooperative Program. Every time your church gives to the work of your state, you are participating in helping victims of natural disasters.

To find out more how you and your church can participate directly including how to be trained to be mobilized, contact your state convention or visit www.namb.net/send-relief

---

in our local community. Likewise, state conventions become the local hub for mission activity in our area and region.

If there's a need to care for the fatherless through adoption or foster care, we jump in. If we can encourage students to grow in Christ while pursuing their academic training, we engage. There's hardly a single church that could take on the whole of the system. As Dr. Paul Chitwood, President of the International Mission Board put it, churches cooperate together so they can accomplish the "large scale functions that are more than what 99 percent of churches can do."[4]

To do more, we partner together.

GEARING UP

My son loves to ride his bike. He rides hundreds of miles enjoying the fresh air, never knowing what adventure lurks around the corner.

His bike is pretty typical: handlebars, a few gears, and, of course, two wheels.

Those wheels look like those on almost every other bike. There's a hub where the wheel attaches to the bike and the spokes that attach to the rim and the tires. These elements work together for a strong and lightweight wheel that gets you where you need to go.

Baptists believe that every individual congregation possesses power through Christ to get where they should go. They can do it through Christ and His strength. But have you ever been cycling up a hill on a single-gear bike? It gets tough! If you have a bike with multiple gears, you change the gear selector and the bike adjusts the gear ratio, making it easier to pedal so you can conquer that hill.

State conventions are like that.

As the church works in the power of Christ to accomplish her calling, the state or regional convention gives churches an extra gear to do more. Through their resourcing, these conventions help churches create margin to do more—more church planting, more effective outreach, more with missions, more of the kingdom. The state or regional convention leaders in your area are your regional missionaries!

How is this possible?

It's because churches of all sizes work together to do the work of the ministry. Together, we give each other an extra gear to accomplish more. The state convention is designed to be a finely tuned hub that enables the churches to do their work efficiently, effectively, and cooperatively.

Individual churches make up each regional convention. These individual churches, partnered together, make a difference on the regional level. They provide the "next gear" to maximize ministry.

So what specifically do they do?

Identify Opportunities. Our convention staff work as lead missionaries on behalf of the churches to help us coordinate more strategically for the sake of the mission. They know the pulse of the state and the region and point out opportunities for the local churches.

This is an important point—we do not have a hierarchy in Baptist life in which our regional leaders tell our local churches what to do. Our leaders work with churches to point out opportunities to be seized by the local congregations while at the same time listening to local pastors and church leaders about local needs. This partnership enables churches to remain autonomous while accomplishing amazing things that are more than one, single congregation could ever do alone.

As the state or regional conventions see and hear of unique opportunities for evangelism and the advance of the gospel, they move quickly to help churches seize the moment.

Because of this, one of their key roles is to facilitate churches starting new churches and to train potential church planters. They help congregations identify new growth areas in the region that might be a perfect place to start a new congregation. Many of these new congregations are creative new ministries that are reaching and baptizing more new believers.

Increasingly, regional leaders help congregations know about opportunities for church planting, especially with ethnic groups due to shifting, global immigration patterns. The world is arriving in the United States, and we can impact their community here and even whole family units back in their native countries as we see them come to Christ.

Strengthen the Church. Sometimes churches struggle. Perhaps you've been a part of a congregation that split over an issue in the church. Maybe the church lost its fire for evangelism or its mission focus, and it plateaued and slowly begins to die. In moments of crisis or challenge, regional leaders are there to help congregations get back on their feet.

Regional or state convention leaders help congregations during these times to refocus on what is essential in ministry. They help them connect to demographic resources and point congregations toward a new vision of reaching their community for

Christ. These leaders prepare churches for engaging their communities afresh so that more people come to know Christ.

Every network of churches has some level of connectivity. Maybe it is a specific church-growth strategy or some other practical approach to ministry. But since methods change over the years, the strongest connection between churches is a shared theological vision. For state conventions, the shared theological vision is located in the *Baptist Faith and Message*. They provide congregations with a claim of "we believe this together."

Since the seventeenth century Baptist churches used faith statements, often known as "confessions," to communicate clearly to others about the biblical claims of faith. You don't often find Baptists questioning the core beliefs of their faith or the moral outworking of those claims. Beautifully crafted, these confessions allow Baptists to hold to the essentials while functioning as independent entities. As congregations work together, they know that every church in their network has the same core beliefs, but they might have different worship or preaching styles.

Make a Difference. State and regional conventions are uniquely designed to make a difference structurally in our culture. Many conventions have a person who actively monitors legislative actions in our states that might have an impact on religious liberty. Many regions help local churches invest in fulfilling our James 1:8 mandate to meet the needs of widows and orphans through retirement homes and facilities that help with foster care and adoption. In many regions Baptists working together even started hospitals and health care organizations!

Reach and Train the Next Generation. On staff at every regional convention are specialists who help equip congregations to reach the next generation for Christ. They host trainings on more effective evangelism through the local church. They know how to tweak Bible study structures for more effective outreach. Want a better kids or youth program? They have great, practical helps for your congregation and can resource your congregation to make a difference for the future.

Connect College Students to Jesus. One of the more amazing investments that many state conventions make is in our Baptist university structures. These colleges, founded with an eye to unique Baptist principles, enable graduates to make an impact in their vocation as well as in their local church. Our Baptist Colleges and Universities commitment to biblical truth equips an entire generation to effectively engage a lost world. For students who choose a non-Baptist university, our regional conventions provide for missionaries on major campuses that equip college students in evangelism and nurture their faith during their academic journey. This happens through partnerships with local churches, the Baptist Student Union, or Baptist Collegiate Ministries.

Train in Evangelism and Discipleship. As part of a broader, shifting culture, how can we connect people with the good news of Jesus Christ? Our state convention leaders work to help congregations share Jesus effectively with our communities and develop

> *College. Freshman year. Rebecca's faith was in crisis. She grew up in the church, but alone in her dorm room she realized she didn't have a real relationship with God. A fellow freshman invited her to the Baptist Collegiate Ministry at Syracuse. There she experienced God's grace for the first time. She understood what it meant to know Him. Her story is not isolated, but the testimony of thousands.*

new Christ-followers. Whether it's through a Youth Evangelism Conference or a reminder of the power of Sunday school to win hearts to Christ, these convention leaders enable churches to do more than they could ever do alone.

WHAT ABOUT ASSOCIATIONS?

Local church associations take the principles of the State or Regional convention and work through an even tighter geographic lens. They often support camps, help coordinate pulpit supply for small congregations, and serve as local liaisons for churches. In some cities they are the first place that churches or state conventions may look to strategically think through where new outreach or church planting might need to happen. As the needs are identified, the leaders in the association help identify congregations who can meet that local need.

It's another way for congregations to serve one another and their community. Even more than the state or regional convention, the association can be the main connection point for pastors to fellowship and encourage one another. It's also a way for congregations to occasionally connect their youth or kid's ministries together for a time of fellowship. This helps us all realize that we are part of something much bigger than ourselves!

Not every area or region has a local association. And state or regional conventions interact with associations in different ways. Like much of Baptist life, the local churches drive what is accomplished, and that's why associations have almost as wide of variety as the local churches they serve. That's why it's possible that your congregation supports both the state or regional convention *and* the local association, or maybe they bypass the associational level all together.

When we think how this works, often our giving looks like this:

State Convention:
- Baptist Universities
- Baptist Children's Home
- Baptist Disaster Relief
- State/Regional Leadership Development
- State/Regional Evangelism and Missions Strategy
- State/Regional Church Planting Coordination
- Liaisons with North American Mission Board and IMB
- Mobilizers for Missions in the State and beyond
- Lobbying and Protecting religious liberty in the political sphere
- Coordinators for National and Global engagement through the National Southern Baptist Convention

Association:
- Local Ministry
- Local Church Planting
- Local Cooperation
- Local Connection

Ministry starts in the local church and radiates from there to the association and the state convention. When a congregation gives through the Cooperative Program to its state or regional convention, approximately half of those dollars go to support the regional ministries that we share together.

SUPPORTING THE WORK TOGETHER

When we talk "Cooperative Program," we understand giving through this channel. Dollars originate in the local church for ministry because, in Baptist life, the local church is always the primary ministry setting. Since each church is autonomous, a congregation works internally to establish the level of support they believe to be the best investment for the future.

Each local church designates a percentage of their general offering receipts, which they then give to help the broader work of the ministry. This work we do *together* is the Cooperative Program. It is the most powerful tool at our disposal to effectively accomplish the broader calling our churches have to reach the lost for Christ. The resources we share enable us to consistently make a difference in our community and beyond.

The Cooperative Program is Southern Baptists' unified plan of giving through which cooperating Southern Baptist churches give a percentage of their undesignated receipts in support of their respective state convention and the Southern Baptist Convention missions and ministries.

Through the Cooperative Program a church can reach their community, their state, North America, and the nations with the gospel

It doesn't matter if a congregation runs twenty, two hundred, or two thousand. Each church working and cooperating *together* makes a difference for reaching our cities, our state, our country, and the world for Jesus Christ.

The best part of this plan is that it starts at home. Cooperative Program giving flows *through* our state and regional conventions. When our congregations give cooperatively, we are equipping our region for the work we have in our own backyards while reaching the world. It's the epitome of, "Think globally, act locally." For congregations, this means our ability to support and uphold our work throughout the world starts right in our own backyards. It's why our giving to the state convention matters—we are taking the first step to reach the world for Christ.

LIVING IT BIBLICALLY

Some have called this the Acts 1:8 strategy. Jesus, speaking to his followers said this:

"But you will receive power when the Holy Spirit has come on you, and you will be my witnesses in Jerusalem, in all Judea and Samaria, and to the end of the earth."

The structure is simple.

Start at home: your Jerusalem. This is where our local churches shine. What are we doing in our own congregations to make a difference?

Move to the regional: your Judea. The state conventions and local associations help us accomplish this critical work.

Impact the nation: your Samaria. Samaria was an adjacent nation in the time of the book of Acts. By moving from our direct region, we can apply the same concept to our neighboring states and, by extension, our nation. We'll talk more about how we accomplish this together in our chapter on North American Mission Board.

Reach your world: to the ends of the earth. No stone is to be left unturned! We have a priority to reach the lost with the gospel. The International Mission Board helps us do just that. Our chapter on the IMB will talk more about the critical work we do together around the world.

Through the Cooperative Program we accomplish the mandate Jesus gave to every believer and every church. We start at home and work together to reach the world for Jesus. As we give to our local church, we empower engagement in our community, in our region, and even to the ends of the earth!

KEY QUESTIONS:

1. How does Acts 1:8 set a model for us to reach the world?

2. Why do Baptists always start with the local church?

3. How do association and state conventions differ?

4. Go to the website for your state convention. What are some ministries in your state convention?

5. Who is on the executive team of your association or state convention? Have your study group pray for these missionaries when you gather.

6. Are there new ministries your church could participate in through your state convention?

CHAPTER 3

HOW YOUR CHURCH CAN CHANGE A NATION

Andrea sat in her divorce attorney's office sobbing. Her husband, Justin, had come home drunk again. He told her he wanted to change, but he never did. She wanted out.

A few miles away, Justin sat in the office of a mentor. John had first become his mentor when Justin came out of rehab years ago. Now he turned to John for help in saving his marriage.

John and Justin picked up the phone and Andrea, at the attorney's office, answered. She asked John, "Does God really still want me to be married to *him*?"

"God is in the business of taking broken things and fixing them," replied John. "Your husband has just given his life to Christ. Please come down to the church, and we'll talk about what's next."

Today, a year later, Justin has been baptized and continues to grow in Christ. Their marriage is as strong as it has ever been. Through John and his church plant, Grace in the City Church in downtown Minneapolis, God has saved a marriage and healed a family.

Pastor John started Grace in the City Church and reached Justin and Andrea because of the funds he receives through Southern Baptists giving to start churches. As Southern Baptists give to the Cooperative Program—and through it to the North American Mission Board—Southern Baptists are starting churches and reaching people like Justin and Andrea with the gospel all across the United States.

Since their founding, Southern Baptists have been committed to sharing the gospel with everyone. Through both what we say and how we live, we want to see the US and Canada transformed through this message.

Previous generations of Baptists faithfully shared the gospel. Yet, the task of reaching North America remains mostly unfinished. Today, nearly 300 million people in the United States and Canada do not know Christ.

COOPERATION: HOW CHURCHES REACH A NATION.

Consider the early church in the book of Acts.

Starting with just one hundred and twenty people gathered in a single room, the church shook the Roman Empire to its very core. Because of the work of a handful of believers, a nation that was almost entirely pagan was transformed by the gospel. How did this happen?

1. First, there was the gospel message the churches proclaimed.
2. Second, there was the Holy Spirit who empowered the work of the churches.
3. Third, there was the agreement between churches to work together.

First, the gospel message. Peter's sermons in Acts 2:14-40 and 3:12-26 exemplify the message proclaimed throughout the book. There Peter proclaimed:

- that Jesus, who had been brutally executed by crucifixion, was the promised Savior;
- that Jesus, who returned from the dead, had overcome death and sin; and
- that those who repented and confessed Jesus would be delivered.

Literally tens of thousands of people in Jerusalem responded. The first church was born. In Acts the gospel message changed a country.

Second, the Spirit's power. To read Acts is to read of the work of the Holy Spirit. It was the Spirit who empowered Peter's preaching on Pentecost and enabled people to hear of God's mighty work in their own languages (2:12). It was the Spirit that led and empowered early church leaders to go to the Samaritans (8:4-17), the God-fearing Gentiles (10:44-48), and then the pagan Gentiles (19:1-7) in rapid succession. It was the Spirit who led to new churches being birthed throughout the Roman Empire.

Third, a cooperating methodology. As the message was proclaimed and the Spirit moved, new churches were formed as men such as Peter and Paul took the gospel throughout the Roman Empire. Yet Acts isn't just a story of the message proclaimed by these Spirit-empowered men. It is also a story of how churches worked together to equip these first missionaries and advance the gospel message through their support for one another.

Consider two examples of this cooperative work between churches. Acts 15 outlines a dispute that arose between Gentile and Jewish believers in the early church. Did the Gentiles in the church in Antioch need to follow the Jewish law and be circumcised? At first glance, this controversy appears to be about rules. But it was deeply missional. Did Gentiles need to become Jews to follow Jesus?

The decision? The Gospel is for everyone. The church in Jerusalem advised the church in Antioch to abstain from idolatry and immorality, but they didn't need to follow the law and be circumcised.

The result? In Acts 16:4-5 missionary teams led by Paul and Barnabas were sent out from the existing churches with this message that the gospel included the Gentiles. New churches were started, and many more people came to follow Jesus.

When churches in a nation work together to reach their nation they send out people who share the gospel, see people converted, and start new churches.

Acts 11 illustrates a second way that churches cooperate with one another. The new church in Antioch had learned that a famine was coming and that Judea and Jerusalem would be hit hard. What did they do? Everyone, according to their individual ability, gave "to send relief to their brothers." Paul and Barnabas then took their gifts to those in Judea and Jerusalem.

When churches in a nation work together to reach their nation, they pool their resources to meet the needs of those in crisis.

For churches to transform North America, the message of the gospel must be proclaimed to everyone, a movement of God will have to take place as we depend on God to empower our message, and we must have a methodology that brings people and churches together to reach our country.

THE NORTH AMERICAN MISSION BOARD: A TOOL FOR REACHING A NATION

Just as no one church could reach the Roman Empire, no one church can reach North America.

For the gospel to transform the United States and Canada, we will have to work together. This is where the North American Mission Board (NAMB) fits in.

NAMB brings churches together in a two-pronged strategy to send out Christians to transform North America with the gospel: The Send Network and the Send Relief program.

SEND NETWORK

Just as Paul and Barnabas were sent out from churches to reach the Roman Empire, Southern Baptists partner together to send out church planters like John to the cities of North America to start churches. Proclaiming the same gospel message and depending upon the same Holy Spirit, NAMB church planters are steadily pushing back darkness and changing our nation.

Southern Baptists have worked together from their very earliest days to plant churches in those areas where there were few Bible-preaching churches. In the very first report of the Domestic Mission Board (now NAMB), the need for missionaries in "the capitals and chief commercial towns as yet unprovided for [including] Little Rock, Arkansas, Austin and St. Antonio in Texas, and Baton Rouge, LA."[5]

Today, Southern Baptists build on this legacy of evangelism and church planting through the Send Network. The Send Network identifies, trains, and supports church planters to plant churches in areas where

> **Get Involved**
>
> The American South and Midwest have far higher concentrations of evangelical Christians than other parts of North America. State conventions in these stronger regions form partnerships to send churches on mission trips to those regions of North America in greater need. Contact your state convention for information on how you can get involved.

gospel need is greatest. With over 80 percent of the population of North America living in cities, NAMB has identified the thirty-two urban areas with the highest number of people in need of a gospel witness.

In most of these cities there is a desperate need for more evangelistic work, for more gospel witnesses, and for more churches. To reach these communities NAMB makes a multi-year commitment to resourcing and equipping church planters and their church plants. Through the Cooperative Program Southern Baptists resource these planters so they are never alone in the work of church planting. To learn more about the Send Network, church planting, and to become part of the church planting process, check out www.namb.net/send-network.

SEND RELIEF

Not only is NAMB committed to starting and equipping churches to share the gospel with their neighbors, it is also committed to resourcing you and your church as your live out the gospel in your community.

The New Testament continually confronts its readers with the reality that the gospel is to be *both* proclaimed *and* lived out. We've already noted how early Christian churches worked together across the vast spans of the Roman Empire to send relief to churches and people in need. James the brother of Jesus reminded early Christians that religion that is pure and undefiled before God is to visit orphans and widows in their affliction and to keep oneself unstained from the world (James 1:27).

Many people in North America have massive physical needs. NAMB's second division, Send Relief both equips and brings together churches to care for those in and at their point of greatest need. They conduct this work in partnership with state conventions and their social ministries. This work creates opportunities for gospel witness, sharing the gospel, and demonstrating the Christian religion, resulting in and people being born again.

Send Relief specifically seeks to meet physical needs in five areas while equipping churches and individuals to share the gospel.

Poverty. Send Relief provides resources and networks for churches to impact poverty in their community. Specifically, resources for you and your church to address hunger, homelessness, illiteracy, and even medical needs in your community are available at https://www.sendrelief.org/poverty/.

Human Trafficking. Modern slavery. Adults and children are being sold in every city and town in the United States. Baptists are working together to end this horrible practice. Through shelters, churches, and ministry leaders, we are seeking to identify those being trafficked and to provide them with a safe way out.[6]

Refugees & Internationals. They come here seeking safety, a better life, a new start. Through ESL, poverty-relief, prayer, and a host of other resources, Send Relief provides practical tools to help churches reach out to those who come here in search of a better

---

Tammy's Story

The doorbell rang. Tammy, a sixteen-year-old girl, could barely stand in the entrance of the Baptist Friendship House. She hadn't eaten or slept in three days and collapsed the minute she was invited in.

Tammy had been experiencing difficulties at home. She felt lonely, unseen, and unheard, until she was befriended on social media. A trafficker had found her and learned about her weaknesses. He pretended to be Tammy's boyfriend. The trafficker in disguise bought Tammy a bus ticket to New Orleans, met her at the station, took her to Bourbon Street, and got her drunk.

The next morning she awoke in an abandoned house, where multiple people were inducing her and others with drugs. They planned on selling the girls during a big event in the city later that day.

But Tammy happened to stumble across the Baptist Friendship House doorstep, looking for a bathroom. She was circling death but was given something to eat and some serious advice. Counselors sat with her and watched over her while she napped because she had been afraid to sleep alone. They arranged for a safe way to get her out of danger and to get her home with resources to start fresh.

---

life. Take a look at https://www.sendrelief.org/ refugees-internationals/ for more information on how you and your church can reach out to those newly here.

Foster Care and Adoption. NAMB works with church and state convention partners to provide resources to create a culture of adoption in churches.

Disaster Response. Send Relief brings churches and state conventions together to quickly and efficiently deploy people and resources to areas struck by natural disaster. For more on this work, see the last chapter.

ANNIE ARMSTRONG: HOW ONE WOMAN SPARKED A MISSIONS MOVEMENT

First, there was the home for destitute children. They needed beds, meals, and education. Annie gave selflessly and brought many of the children to Sunday School at her church. Next there were those coming out of the jails who needed jobs and the Lord. Annie raised funds, found opportunities, and brought missionaries into the lives of these ex-convicts. Then there was the school for Native American children. They didn't have any clothes. Who would help them? Next there was the local orphanage with overcrowding. Then there was the missionary working with African-Americans who needed funding. The missional needs of her community were tremendous. Her church and the other ladies in it were committed to impacting their community with the gospel. But they couldn't do it alone.

Annie was relentless. She went from church to church, women's group to women's group, raising funds, telling the story of the gospel need.

Annie knew that the call to change her community, the call to change her country, with the gospel wasn't just a call for her pastor, or even for her church; it was a call for all churches to embrace. As a result, she began to network the women's groups in not only her church but in churches throughout the country. Never taking a salary, she started the Women's Missionary Union. It's goal: to raise awareness and funds for missions throughout North America. For Annie, missions was everybody's responsibility.

Today we honor her work through the collection of the Annie Armstrong Easter Offering for North American Missions. Every dollar collected through this offering goes to support the work of missionaries throughout North America working to plant churches and send relief to those area in greatest need.

Additionally, the Women's Missionary Union she founded provides programs and educational resources to churches to inform and connect churches and individuals to the mission work. You can learn more about the WMU at www.wmu.com

HOW YOU AND YOUR CHURCH CAN CHANGE OUR NATION

Annie was committed to changing first her city, her state, and her country with the gospel. We want to challenge you to connect with your state convention and NAMB to change our country. The task of reaching North America is bigger than you and your church, but you are not alone in this task. Through NAMB and your state convention you can:

1. Connect to churches in the less-reached, less-evangelized parts of North America. Through your state convention you can

partner with churches in other parts of the country and go on a short-term mission trip. Through NAMB you can connect with a Send City Coordinator to see how your church can serve a church planter or re-planter.

2. Partner with church planters. We want to challenge you to not only go on mission with planters but also to be a sending church. Send resources, people, and prayer to a church in need of resources. For more see https://www.namb.net/church-mobilization

3. Send relief to those in greatest need. The Send Relief website provides a host of ways for you and your church to connect with those at times of crisis and at points of need. Check out www.sendrelief.org

4. Support the work of reaching North America. The early church changed an empire with the gospel through its message, the Holy Spirit, and their cooperative work. As you pray for missionaries, as you give through the Cooperative Program and the Annie Armstrong Offering, as you go and share both in your community and throughout North America, you push back the lostness and advance the gospel.

KEY QUESTIONS:

1. The task of reaching North America begins with the gospel message we are all to share. What are some ways you can share the gospel in your circles of influence?

2. If you don't have a method for sharing the Gospel, take a look at this video from NAMB on a practical way to share Christ: https://www.namb.net/video/3-circles-life-conversation-guide

3. This chapter has challenged you to think about why churches should work together. What do you think happens when churches don't work together? What would happen if you and your church cooperated with other churches more through an entity like NAMB?

4. The physical needs of people in North America are massive. Take a look at one of these resources from NAMB:

    1) On Refugees: https://www.sendrelief.org/w-content/uploads/2018/03/NAMB17-Ebook-Refugees-FINAL-FM.pdf. Take a look at page 14 for ways to help

    2) On Foster Care and Adoption: https://www.sendrelief.org/wp-content/uploads/edd/2018/02/

NAMB17-SendRelief-Adoption-Ebook.pdf. Take a look at page 9 for ways to help.

3) On Poverty: https://www.sendrelief.org/poverty/. Take a look at the Arise2Read page and backpacks of hope links for some practical ideas.

5. Discuss how you and your small group/church can implement one of these ideas to meet needs in your community. Develop a plan and work with your small group/church to meet this need.

6. Check out the website for the WMU: www.wmu.com. In examining these resources, what are some ways you can promote missions in your church?

CHAPTER 4

HOW YOUR CHURCH CAN CHANGE THE NATIONS

June 2017: Thousands of Southern Baptists gathered in the convention hall to hear the annual report from the International Mission Board (IMB). Story after story of global, gospel impact reverberated through the hall. The room was electric. Who doesn't get excited hearing about people from all over the globe coming to faith in Jesus?

Following the report the leader of the IMB invited questions from those attending.

That's when Kambiz Saghaey stood.

"I don't have a question," he stated. Instead, "I want to say thank you. Because you came, I heard the gospel, and God saved me and my family and through us many others. . . . I want to say thank you to all Southern Baptist churches because you send, because you support, God changed a fanatic Muslim to an ordained pastor."

You could have heard a pin drop in that room with over 5,000 people. What a story! Saghaey continued, "We need your prayer. Please pray for us. We are a member of your family . . . to reach the world and reach the Muslims."

This story has been repeated in many different ways since 1845. That year, Southern Baptists came together and started their convention "in one Sacred Effort, for the propagation of the Gospel . . . to promote foreign and domestic missions."[7]

For over 170 years the Southern Baptist Convention has been doing just that.

Many might even say the driving concern and unifying force for the SBC has been the sending of missionaries. By cooperating together and pooling our resources, the IMB empowers churches to send missionaries to take the gospel to those who have never heard of Jesus. In partnering with the IMB, you and your church change the nations and in turn, the entire world.

WHY THE NATIONS? CHRIST'S MANDATE

Telling the world about Jesus has always been part of the mandate to believers.

- In Matthew Jesus commands the apostles to "go to all the nations and make disciples." (Matt 28:19)

- In Mark, they are told to go into all the world and proclaim the Gospel. (Mark 16:15)
- In Luke repentance and forgiveness are to be proclaimed to all nations. (Luke 24:47)
- In John Jesus sends out his disciples in the Spirit with a message of peace. (John 20:21)
- In Acts Jesus tells them to be His witnesses in Jerusalem, Judea, Samaria, and to the ends of the earth. (Acts 1:8)

For Jesus's followers there was no doubt. Followers of Jesus tell others about Jesus. We proclaim the good news of the gospel, of Jesus's perfect life, of His substitutionary death for sin, of His life-giving resurrection, and of His claim of absolute Lordship so that everyone would hear, repent, and believe in Him. Jesus always intended for the gospel to go to all the nations and peoples, to go even to those who were at the very ends of the earth.

YOU AND THE NATIONS

Who did Jesus call to the nations? You

In Matthew 28:18–20 Jesus commands those gathered to go and make disciples of *all* nations. He then promises to empower us to do this *until the end of the age.*

There are still unreached people groups who have never heard the name of Jesus.

Jesus hasn't returned yet.

So...

There is no expiration date on the Great Commission.

You and I are called to make disciples of all nations.

But how? Just consider the size of the task of bringing the gospel to the nations. There are over 2.8 billion people who do not even have access to the gospel. There are over 3,000 people groups that are completely unreached. "The greatest injustice in the world is that thousands of people groups, representing billions of people, are on a path that leads to an eternal hell, and no one has even told them how they could go to heaven."[8] Yet you could spend the rest of your life telling people how to go to heaven and barely impact global lostness.

> A people group is the largest group of people within which the gospel could flow freely without running up against a significant barrier such as ethnic identity, language, religion, culture, shared history, and/or geography. There are far more people groups in the world than there are political countries.

YOUR CHURCH AND THE NATIONS

But God never intended for you to reach the nations alone. Taking the Gospel to and making disciples of the nations *begins* with you, but it isn't *just* for you.

To go to the nations means that both you and your church are called to make disciples of all peoples. You and your church are called to send, finance, and equip one another to go to the nations.

Not only has Jesus called you and your church to the nations, he has also instructed you and your church on what to do when you get there. Specifically, Jesus expects you to:

1. Evangelize the Unreached:

In Matthew 28:19-20, Jesus commands his followers to go to everyone. He is commanding his followers to go to the unreached and evangelize the nations. When we evangelize we literally proclaim Good News. What is that news? It is the gospel itself! Evangelism has the aim of persuading people to repent and believe in Christ. Evangelism is more than mere presentation of the gospel; it is persuasion with the gospel.

2. Disciple the Newly Reached:

Next, you make disciples by teaching converts to observe Christ's commands (Matt 28:20).

How do you teach the nations to follow Christ? To help the nations follow, a missionary must

- learn their language,
- understand their Culture, and
- obtain a proper translation of much of the Bible.

Teaching a people to follow means that someone needs to give their life to that people. It means that you and your church sacrificially give and go to make disciples.

3. Plant and Multiply Churches

Just as you grow into all the Jesus commands you to be through a local church, so do new believers grow into all Jesus commands them to be through a local church. In Ephesians 4 and 1 Corinthians 12, Paul speaks of how each believer submits to Christ through submitting to one another. In the local church, disciples grow into who Christ intends them to be and as a result the entire church grows into the image of Christ. Therefore, to go to the nations means to go start churches and to see that those churches start more churches.

4. Train Leaders

Every church needs leaders. In the United States, churches and seminaries partner together to train leaders. But such is uncommon among the nations and non-existent among the unreached. For your church to make disciples and plant churches, you must also equip leaders who will equip the next generation. This is why Paul told Timothy to train leaders (2 Timothy 2:2). The next generation of disciples depends on indigenous leaders.

This four-fold task of evangelizing the unreached, discipling the newly reached, planting and multiplying churches, and training leaders is the mission of the International Mission Board.

THE IMB: HOW YOU AND YOUR CHURCH CHANGE THE NATIONS

If your church is large, it may be able to make a gospel impact and start churches in one or two nations. Yet the task of evangelizing, teaching, church planting, and training leaders for the nations is beyond any one church. God's plan is for every Christian and every church going to the nations. Only as Christians and their churches work together to take the gospel to the nations does Jesus's command to reach all peoples becomes possible.

Through the International Mission Board, nearly 50,000 churches pool their resources and their members to change the nations. The IMB exists to partner with your church in order to empower missionary teams from your church to evangelize, disciple, plant and multiply healthy churches, and train leaders among the unreached so that there will be "a multitude from every language, people, tribe and nation knowing and worshiping our Lord Jesus Christ."[9] For over 170 years the IMB has worked with churches just like yours to change the nations.

For example, consider the story of an early Southern Baptist missionary.

LOTTIE MOON: HOW SHE CHANGED A NATION

One of our early missionaries gave everything to take the gospel to China. Having been born to a

A Tale of Two Missionaries

The Martins and the Joneses graduated from seminary with the same dream: to serve overseas as missionaries. The Martins prayed about where God would have them go and settled on West Africa. They knew of some missionaries there who had been sent by a well-known agency. They contacted the organization, set up a time to go through the assessment process, and passed their evaluation with flying colors.

Meanwhile, the Joneses felt drawn to a country in Southeast Asia with very few Christians. They applied through the International Mission Board and eventually were matched with an assignment in that region.

The couples started packing around the same time and flew off in different directions. The Joneses headed to the IMB offices for orientation and then on to their mission field. The Martins embarked on a year-long tour of churches in their state, sharing about the work they would soon do and raising the funds that would provide their food, rent, insurance, transportation, and other living expenses.

When back stateside, the Joneses spent a year speaking at conferences and churches, recruiting volunteer teams to pray with them and to serve with them in Southeast Asia. The Martins did some of that, but mostly focused on raising the money they needed to live. Occasionally, they would have to leave their country at a critical time because their financial need was too great.

Both couples shared the gospel with people who had never heard it, lived with similar cross-cultural challenges, and saw people come to Christ. But the Martins were often left alone with a constant pressure to raise money, while the Joneses were never alone and were able to stay on the mission field, focused on their work, because of support they received through the Cooperative Program.

wealthy, historic Virginia family, this was not the life one would have expected for this well-educated debutante and prominent Christian skeptic. Yet after her conversion at eighteen, the gospel message transformed Lottie Moon's life. Recognizing Christ's mandate to the nations, Moon gave her life to missionary service

Arriving in China, she initially struggled. Surrounded by a culture that had little regard for human life, devalued women, and taunted her with calls of "devil-woman" every time she went out, Charlotte "Lottie" Moon endured famines, her sister's departure from the mission field because of poor health, and inadequate funding for the mission work. Yet, because of Christ's mandate she remained.

For over thirty-nine years Lottie gave everything to reach the Chinese people. Confronted with mass illiteracy, she started schools built around the Bible. When famine struck, she gave away her own food. Scorned by locals, she baked cookies for their children. She adopted their clothing style and immersed herself into Chinese culture. Lottie wrote letters home detailing China's hunger for truth and the urgent need for more workers and for Southern Baptists to support them through prayer and giving.

The result of her service? She shared the story of Christ's life, death, and resurrection with thousands. Many became Christians who in turn led many more to Christ. Church planter and evangelist Li Showting became a Christian because of Lottie Moon's witness. He baptized more than ten thousand people during his ministry and founded churches in multiple provinces. Because Lottie toiled in the field, the gospel message multiplied many times over.

Today there are tens of millions of Christians and thousands of house churches in China in part because of the lasting impact of her ministry. With time and commitment, she overcame initial hesitancies to her gospel work and changed a nation with the gospel because churches gave to and supported her work.

WHAT'S NEXT: WAYS YOU AND YOUR CHURCH CHANGE THE NATIONS

We want to challenge you to be part of God's plan for changing the world. Here are a few ways you and you church can change the nations.

Give: Give as a church. Give from your regular church budget to missions through the Cooperative Program. The Cooperative Program contributes nearly $200 million every year to the International Mission Board.

Give personally. You can Give to the Lottie Moon Christmas Offering, 100 percent of which goes to serve the missionaries and their work the world over. It purchases vehicles and computers, leases locations for new church plants, and accomplishes unique projects that are carefully vetted by leaders in the field.

Give sacrificially. In the history of the Southern Baptist Convention, a contribution of 10 percent of a congregation's undesignated receipts was the generally accepted ideal. Many churches give well above that percentage because of the critical work being done worldwide. Your church can make a difference by giving sacrificially to make disciples of all nations.

Partner: Partner with the IMB. Go to https://www.imb.org/for-churches to see a list of ways you and your church can specifically partner with the IMB. Opportunities include short-term mission trips, hosting a missionary, and prayer using a provided list of specific ways to pray.

Partner with your state convention. State convention personnel work to partner churches with missionaries and missions. For smaller churches, they will help coordinate mission trips. They connect churches and associations to missions by bringing in missionaries and offering missions promotions events. (For example, see https://a18c.org/onmissionconnections/)

Partner with the WMU. The WMU provides educational resources and curriculums for the promotion of missions in your Sunday School, small group and church. These resources are tailored to every age. For more see http://www.wmu.com/

Go: Missions is not just for a select few, but for every Christian. Through the CP the number of people who can be on mission is limitless. Every vacation, every business trip, every time you travel is an opportunity to take the gospel with you. The IMB equips professionals to be on mission when they travel overseas. They train students and teachers to go into schools to reach the lost. They have need for retirees who want to go. Still others are needed to give their entire lives to evangelism, discipleship, church planting, and leadership training for the nations. If you are willing to go, the IMB wants to partner with you and your church to reach the ends of the earth.

We have a mandate from Jesus to share the life-giving gospel of Jesus Christ.

Through the Cooperative Program you and your church change the nations with the gospel.

People are evangelized and discipled.

Churches are started and multiplied.

Leaders are trained.

Together we change the nations so that a multitude composed of those from every nation will praise Jesus for all eternity.

A veterinarian, Rebecca, went to Southeast Asia with the IMB to share the gospel. Partnering with a local believing businessman's goat dairy farm, she teaches and practices veterinary medicine by day. In the evening she spends time with locals and shares with them the hope of the gospel.

KEY QUESTIONS:

1. Read Matthew 28:19-20, Mark 16:15, Luke 24:27, John 20:21, and Acts 1:8. Discuss how God plans for the nations to become disciples.

2. Reflect on the tale of two missionaries. What are some of the advantages of doing missions through the Cooperative Program?

3. Go to https://www.imb.org/trips/, https://www.imb.org/opportunity-finder/, and https://www.imb.org/for-churches. What can you do today and the weeks ahead to be part of God's mission to the nations?

4. What should you give or give up in order to take the gospel to the ends of the earth?

CHAPTER 5
HOW YOUR CHURCH CAN CHANGE THE FUTURE

Every Sunday a rag-tag group of kids entered a room decked with chairs, games, and the promise of engaging hearts and minds for the kingdom of God.

Every Sunday dedicated, caring volunteers warmly welcomed kids into the room.

Every Sunday the flannel graph board helped illustrate a Bible story.

Every Sunday missionaries framed the center of prayer time.

Every Sunday the gospel was made clear.

Every. Sunday.

The sights, sounds, and smells of that Sunday school room remain etched in my memory. They were a central fixture in my young adult life that brought together friends and an intentional approach to teaching and training kids, youth, and adults in the knowledge of the Word of God.

There's no way to minimize the value of regularly teaching the Bible week in and week out in the context of the local church. Whether that happens in a traditional classroom or in a small-group setting at someone's home, going deeper into the Word of God is a game-changer in the life of the believer.

Baptist churches always understood that education changes us and changes our future.

How does education change the future?

Through education, Christianity is transmitted from one generation to the next. Consider Deuteronomy 6:4–9:

> Listen, Israel: The LORD our God, the LORD is one. Love the LORD your God with all your heart, with all your soul, and with all your strength. These words that I am giving you today are to be in your heart. Repeat them to your children. Talk about them when you sit in your house and when you walk along the road, when you lie down and when you get up. Bind them as a sign on your hand and let them be a symbol on your forehead. Write them on the doorposts of your house and on your city gates.
> We must pass-on the faith. How?

It starts with knowing God. He is the object of our faith. He is the one who we love. We love Him with our whole being—heart, soul, strength.

Because we love Him—

LifeWay Christian Resources

Motto: *Biblical Solutions for Life*
Key Facts:
- *Produces material for more than 160 countries around the world.*
- *Prints the Christian Standard Bible (CSB), a leading English translation.*
- *Parent to Broadman and Holman Press, Holman Bibles, and B&H Academic, who produce books, Bibles, and resources for individuals, pastors, and students.*
- *Operates the digital Bible and resource platform WordSearch*
- *LifeWay Research produces exclusive data used by pastors, Christian leaders, and church planters to make wise decisions.*

Because our heart overflows—
Because of Him—
We must speak, we must tell, we must teach!

Jesus told us in Luke 6:45 that our mouths speak out of the abundance in our hearts. This is why your life needs to overflow with the goodness of Jesus. We want to talk about and teach Jesus. This is why in Deuteronomy Moses reminded the people to continually repeat the goodness of God to their children. And not just on Sunday mornings, but All. The. Time.

Note the progression:

- Sitting at home—as you are relaxing at home or around the table . . .
- On the road—in the car, or on a jog . . .

- When you lie down—before bedtime and as your family goes to sleep . . .
- When you get up—first thing in the morning . . .

The gospel should permeate the realities of life. Every aspect of it.

But it also should be visible—on your person, on the walls of your home, on the entrances of your buildings. We should constantly be teaching one another and teaching our children about God.

We need educational structures that teach us to love God. When we have them, we are furthering this very mission in opposition to the broader trends of the culture. We are helping the next generation connect with the truths of Scripture at every possible level so that they love the Lord their God with their whole being—heart, soul, strength.

LIFEWAY AND THE PROMISE OF STUDYING GOD'S WORD TOGETHER

From the early 1800s Baptists produced a shared curriculum that churches all over the United States would use. Materials, just like today, focused on helping church members understand the contours of the Bible as a whole while diving into deeper, more focused studies of specific biblical books. In the weekly lessons, leaders were given contextual application that addressed moral and social ills while helping the Christian in his or her individual walk with Christ.

From this historical heritage, LifeWay Christian Resources serves churches of the Southern Baptist Convention and beyond by producing Bible study curriculum along with other resources for believers, including training events, print resources, and both physical and digital retail environments. Churches around the globe use LifeWay materials every week in their congregational educational program.

Since the Great Commission is a mandate for reaching the lost, LifeWay aids churches in effectively making disciples and training them to understand the Bible—". . . teaching them to observe all that I have commanded you" (Matt. 28:20). It's discipleship at the most basic level.

The apostle Paul told his protégé Timothy to "present yourself to God as one approved, a worker who doesn't need to be ashamed, correctly teaching the word of truth" (2 Tim 2:15). The apostle Peter challenged the church to be "ready at any time to give a defense to anyone who asks you for a reason for the hope that is in you" (1 Pet 3:15). These challenges to the early church still resonate today as we fulfill the mandate by Jesus to make disciples of all nations. We have a responsibility to train ourselves and the next generation to follow Jesus fully.

The best place for this to happen is the local church. Left to ourselves, we might have the drive and the passion to study the Bible, but together we glean so much more. By joining together as the body of believers in our local church, we see the consistent spiritual growth beyond our own personal, narrow frame of reference. We join with others to pray, serve, and go to the nations with the gospel.

In addition to curriculum for weekly studies, LifeWay encourages individual believers through the resources available at their local LifeWay Christian Store. At these stores, LifeWay curates the best of Christian materials for individual and congregational growth.

As part of their training mission, LifeWay also publishes books that help individual Christians grow in their faith through Broadman and Holman and B&H Academic. These books bring fiction and non-fiction titles designed to encourage hearts, equip Christians, and prepare the next generation of church leaders. These books, Bible studies, and resources can all be found online at www.LifeWay.com.

But LifeWay's work doesn't stop there. They produce research and study materials that help individuals and churches experience growth by better analyzing their neighborhoods and mission fields through LifeWay Research. By revealing common attitudes in the broader culture as well as national trends in church life, pastors and church leaders can make better decisions for how to do more strategic outreach in their neighborhoods. Their church toolkits help congregations move toward spiritual health and effectiveness. Their website connects leaders with the necessary helps to effect lasting, gospel-oriented change in their congregation. You can connect with these tools at www.LifeWayresearch.com.

COLLEGES AND THE PROMISE OF THINKING TOGETHER

What institution stands at the intersection of culture and discipleship?

It's the university!

Christians with a passion to reach the lost and make an impact on the world at large have always understood the broader training and education that needs to happen in the lives of young adults. Thousands of students from around the globe attend Southern Baptist colleges and universities supported by the local churches, their association, and their state convention.

You can imagine the impact! Every year these colleges produce graduates who have spent four years or more in a gospel-oriented environment while training to excel in their chosen fields. These graduates come back to invest in our local churches, in our communities, and around the world through their desired field of study.

This is precisely why early Baptist congregations started universities

From the Campus to The World

At the conclusion of a university mission trip to El Salvador, twenty-one students from Truett-McConnell in Georgia sat in a circle reflecting on God's work in the lives of the Salvadorian people. Students, faculty, and staff saw 627 salvations during their weeklong trip living out their training. "I'll never be the same," one said; "My life is forever changed," echoed another.

that embraced our shared Baptist values to train and educate the next generation.[10]

In 1762 Baptists gathered in Philadelphia at a regional meeting asked for a suitable university. The design was simple: create a university and seminary to train pastors and community leaders in an environment where religious liberty was championed. Since the highest concentration of Baptists in any state at the time was in Rhode Island, Baptists chose to invest in that state, founding "Rhode Island College" in the spring of 1764. Later known as Brown University, this was only the seventh university founded in the United States. While Brown University no longer adheres to its founding principles, we can still see how integral formal education ventures were to Baptists.

Baptists knew that if they would work together, they could provide excellent training for college and seminary students. This passion carried forward into the westward expansion of America. As state conventions formed, they looked for ways to provide for the education of young adults. Alabama Baptists worked hard to start new work. In 1838, they started Judson College, a women's college, with the intent of educating women to be world changers. A few years later, in 1841, Alabama Baptists founded a separate men's college that became known as Samford University. In some instances Baptists took over failed attempts by the state itself. Schools like Union University in Jackson, TN, and Mississippi College in Clinton, MS, took over preexisting schools and reinvigorated their curriculum with Christian values and academic vigor.

State and Local Partnership Matters: Today Southern Baptists fund, endorse, or officially connect with forty-eight colleges and universities as part of their mission to train and educate the coming generations for kingdom service. While the SBC works on a national level to fund theological education, these colleges and universities are part of the work of state conventions. These institutions provide outstanding academic excellence with a Christian worldview and, because of partnerships with your local church, they often are more affordable than your regional state university.

While not every state convention has a university or college affiliated with their work, these forty-eight institutions rely on the generosity of churches giving through the Cooperative Program in their state. These same schools also receive their trustees in part or in full from the state conventions, making them a fantastic, ongoing investment by Baptists for the future.

These same colleges reinvest into their state partnerships through camps for teens and children in the summer, by sending college students into hard-work areas in the state or abroad, and by training lay leaders in congregations how to better serve their community. These schools need our ongoing support both personally and congregationally as Baptists seek to make a difference for the future. You can find out more about each one in your region by visiting the campus or checking out their website. It's another way congregations, through their state conventions show that we work better together!

SCHOOL NAME	STATE CONVENTION	YEAR FOUNDED	WEBSITE
Judson College	AL	1838	http://www.judson.edu/
Samford University	AL	1841	https://www.samford.edu/
University of Mobile	AL	1961	https://umobile.edu/
Williams Baptist College	AR	1941	http://www.wbcoll.edu/
Ouachita Baptist University	AR	1886	https://obu.edu/
California Baptist University	CA	1950	https://calbaptist.edu/
Baptist College of Florida	FL	1913	http://www.baptistcollege.edu/
Brewton-Parker College	GA	1904	http://www.bpc.edu/
Shorter University	GA	1873	http://www.shorter.edu/
Truett McConnell University	GA	1946	https://truett.edu/
Clear Creek Baptist College	KY	1926	https://www.ccbbc.edu/
Georgetown College	KY	1829	http://www.georgetowncollege.edu/
University of the Cumberlands	KY	1913	https://www.ucumberlands.edu/
Louisiana College	LA	1906	http://www.lacollege.edu/
Blue Mountain College	MS	1873	http://www.bmc.edu/
Mississippi College	MS	1826	https://www.mc.edu/
William Carey University	MS	1911	https://www.wmcarey.edu/
Southwest Baptist University	MO	1878	https://www.sbuniv.edu/
Hannibal-LaGrange University	MO	1928	http://www.hlg.edu/
Yellowstone Christian College	MT	1974	https://yellowstonechristian.edu/
Davis College	NY, endorsed by PA, NJ	1900	https://www.davisny.edu/
Campbell University	NC	1887	https://www.campbell.edu/
Chowan University	NC	1848	https://www.chowan.edu/
Fruitland Baptist Bible College	NC	1899	http://www.fruitland.edu/
Mars Hill University	NC	1856	https://www.mhu.edu/
Gardener-Webb University	NC	1905	http://gardner-webb.edu/
Wingate University	NC	1896	https://www.wingate.edu/
Oklahoma Baptist University	OK	1910	https://www.okbu.edu/

SCHOOL NAME	STATE CONVENTION	YEAR FOUNDED	WEBSITE
Anderson University	SC	1911	https://www.anderson-university.edu/
Houston Baptist University	BGCTX	1960	https://www.hbu.edu/
Howard Payne University	BGCTX	1889	http://www.hputx.edu/
Jacksonville College	SBCTX	1899	http://www.jackson-ville-college.edu/
University of Mary Hardin-Baylor	BGCTX	1845	http://www.umhb.edu/
Wayland Baptist University	BGCTX	1908	https://www.wbu.edu/

SEMINARIES AND THE PROMISE OF THEOLOGICAL EDUCATION

As the Baptist family continued to grow and expand, some individuals called for a nationally funded seminary to specifically train pastors and church leaders for the plethora of newly established congregations. This would be very different than the colleges since the training would specifically be for ministers, missionaries, and those dedicated to advancing the cause of the church.

A key voice in this movement was a man named James P. Boyce. Back in 1859 he proposed starting a seminary funded by contributions across the United States that would enable students from all walks of life to engage in ministry studies. He suggested that the seminary should be a place of robust engagement with the Bible, theology, and practical ministry.

With all the attacks in that era on biblical authority and orthodoxy, Boyce suggested that the seminary have a shared statement of faith that served as the main point of cooperation for the institution. All faculty and administrators would need to agree to these basic tenants of faith to provide maximum fidelity and accountability to the churches of the convention.

With these ground rules, The Southern Baptist Theological Seminary opened its doors in South Carolina. After the Civil War, the school relocated to Louisville, KY, where it continues to serve congregations today by training leaders.

But Southern Seminary was only the start. Ever mindful of church and missions needs around the world, Southern Baptists founded five additional seminaries. In total, the six seminaries funded by the Cooperative Program train around 18,000 men and women every year. Thanks to churches who participate in the strategic giving of the Cooperative Program, all Southern Baptist students at these seminaries receive a significant reduction in their tuition that makes their training affordable; many students graduate without student-loan debt.

This affordability framework is yet another way the SBC invests in the task of missions. With students having little to no debt, they can be mobilized to be sent out by the International Mission Board or the North American Mission Board much sooner! Your church, in supporting the Cooperative Program, trains the next generation of *global* leaders!

SEMINARY	YEAR FOUNDED	LOCATION	WEBSITE
The Southern Baptist Theological Seminary	1859	Louisville, KY	www.sbts.edu
Southwestern Baptist Theological Seminary	1908	Fort Worth, TX	www.swbts.edu
New Orleans Baptist Theological Seminary	1917	New Orleans, LA	www.nobts.edu
Gateway Seminary	1944	Ontario, CA	www.gs.edu
Southeastern Baptist Theological Seminary	1950	Wake Forest, NC	www.sebts.edu
Midwestern Baptist Theological Seminary	1957	Kansas City, MO	www.mbts.edu

In addition to operating graduate-level training, most of the seminaries also offer undergraduate programs designed to train younger students as well as adult learners who have not completed their college degree. Perfect for pastors who may be bi-vocational, our colleges can make the difference between a church leader with no education or a church leader with a solid grounding in the Word of God.

But there's even more available for you and your church through our seminaries! With the advent of the internet, all of the SBC seminaries now offer online educational opportunities. These courses help existing pastors train without ever leaving their home congregations. It also enables church members to grow in their knowledge of the Bible and theology in order to serve their community better. You can take an undergraduate or graduate course and grow in your faith!

Because Jesus told the church we were to make disciples by "teaching them to observe everything I have commanded you" (Matt 28:20), the Southern Baptist Convention through the genius of the

Cooperative Program funds educational aspects that touch the lives of individuals through LifeWay Christian Resources. We invest together through our state conventions in the colleges and universities in our region, and nationally we fund our seminaries training future pastors, leaders, and missionaries.

When it comes to growing and following Christ, we are never alone. We work together to fulfill the mandates of Jesus! We are better together!

KEY QUESTIONS:

1. If I understand God calling me to go deeper in my faith, how can I find resources for that?

2. How does LifeWay empower Christians to follow Jesus?

3. Why does investing in Southern Baptist Colleges and Universities matter for the long-term?

4. How does investment in our seminaries matter for our local churches? What about our work through missions?

5. What is the SBC college and seminary closest to you? Find out who the presidents of these schools are. Commit to praying for them and their leadership team. Perhaps send them a note telling them you are praying for the success of their work.

6. Consider how your congregation can provide quality education through student scholarships. Investing in the future always makes a difference.

CHAPTER 6

HOW YOUR CHURCH CAN CHANGE THE CULTURE

Walking in the Wilderness . . .
Jeannine sat at the kitchen table with her head in her hands. After what seemed like an interminable debate with Katie, her daughter, Jeannine had no idea what to do. They raised Katie right—made sure she was in church weekly, read the Bible as a family, even dined together as a whole family—but Katie just let her mom know a dark secret. A few weeks ago, fearing what her parents' reaction would be, Katie made a personal choice and ended a pregnancy she didn't want. Jeannine began to sob, not knowing how to process this burden.

Phil worked tirelessly to build a business reflecting his quest for excellence in artistic expression. For over twenty years he was the leading wedding photographer in his community, but with the changing of the times, he increasingly found himself turning down requests for same-sex weddings. While he happily took pictures of all types of individuals, couples, and families, he didn't think it would be consistent with his faith to participate in a wedding ceremony that didn't match biblical standards.

Last year, the main wedding vendor convention in town banned him from being an advertiser based on his understanding of marriage. Just last month a gay couple asked him to take their wedding photos, but when he said it would in conflict with his beliefs, the couple became irritated and threatened to sue for discrimination. Phil wondered how he would be able to financially sustain his business or his family if this pattern continued. How could he stay faithful to his Christianity and work through this?

Michael and Anne sat in their bedroom not knowing exactly how to feel. Their grandson popped by earlier in the evening and had a great time with them around the dinner table. As he left for the evening, he passed them a note and asked them to carefully read it. He pledged his love for them and walked out the door. Michael and Anne opened the envelope to discover their grandson no longer desired to be known as Chris, but by his preferred name, Christine. He informed them he would be undergoing extensive surgery over the next six months to reconcile his physical appearance with a gender that corresponded to his identity. Michael and Anne were shell-shocked.

Life in the twenty-first century is complex. A couple of generations ago, who would have thought we would be dealing with questions of bio-medically reengineering humans, changing standards on marriage, shifts in cultural understanding of gender, or overt attacks on Christianity itself? Even the political sphere seems crazy, with candidates pulling toward extremes on either side.

It's easy in the ever-changing cultural debates to feel as if you or your church are isolated. Many congregations may even start turning away from engaging their community out of fear of what may happen in the future or through the legal system.

WHY SHOULD WE STILL CARE ABOUT OUR CULTURE?

We love people. Because we love people, we long for them to experience the truths of the gospel, which will lead to their personal flourishing.

But not everyone agrees. In fact, by promoting the truths of the Bible, we can often find ourselves in opposition to the broader culture.

Think about where the Bible's standard is radically different from the broader culture:

- marriage: one man, one woman, for life;
- sexuality: designed for marriage alone;
- gender: God created both genders with unique aspects to reveal his glory.

So what should we do with these and other issues? The apostle Peter helped the early church wrestle with some of the same issues. In 1 Peter 3:14-16, he wrote:

". . . Do not fear what they fear or be intimidated, but in your hearts regard Christ the Lord as holy, ready at any time to give a defense to anyone who asks you for a reason for the hope that is in you. Yet do this with gentleness and respect."

We can't run from culture.

We can't remove ourselves from engaging the culture.

We can't back down from culture. Why?

Because we have truth from the Creator! We stand on a firm foundation!

But when we are feeling the pressure of culture, we often feel overwhelmed. Just like Peter walking on the surface of the water started sinking when he took his eyes off of Christ, we can look at what's going on in the culture and feel like it's too much. But Peter reminds us that our focus must be on Jesus! We are to "regard Christ the Lord." The picture Peter paints for us is that when we trust Jesus as Lord in our hearts, we know we can face any storm. He gives us the strength!

As Jesus gives us the strength, we engage. We give a defense of the hope that is in us! We address the burning issues of the culture with the truth of Jesus!

But how?

Through the Ethics and Religious Liberty Commission of the Southern Baptist Convention.

They equip you and your church to be able to talk effectively about how the gospel relates to all areas of life and culture. They work hard to ensure that even complex questions receive clear, biblical answers.

And they do this with the gentleness and respect the text demands of us. As the ERLC does its work, they seek to be as winsome as possible.

That's hard, especially when the truth of Jesus stands in opposition to dominant waves of culture.

As kingdom people who understand the love of Jesus, we keep sharing truth, engaging the culture and world as we can, and inviting people to come to a Savior who loves them deeply.

HELPING YOU COUNT THE COST

The Ethics and Religious Liberty Commission of the Southern Baptist Convention (ERLC) exists for you and your local church. They serve as a voice for believers and the Southern Baptist Convention within the political sphere while helping us think through the tough questions being raised by our culture. Everything from bio-medical engineering to questions about life are addressed by the staff of the ERLC.

The outward-facing work of the staff of the ERLC lets your church's voice be heard on a national level. Since the Southern Baptist Convention includes over 47,000 churches, we represent a large segment of the population of America. The ERLC takes the voice of the convention reflected at the national meeting and projects that towards Pennsylvania Avenue, Wall Street, and even your local state capitol. Current leaders at the ERLC are sought out by

---

Psalm 139 Project: Every Life Matters

One of the ongoing projects for the ERLC's team in defending the sanctity of human life is to resource pregnancy centers around the United States with ultrasound technology. These ultrasounds show clearly that the child in the womb is exactly that – a child. Since the ERLC works to promote values that favor life, the Psalm 139 Project funnels 100 percent of gifts toward procuring this vital resource to crisis pregnancy centers saving one life at a time.

For it was you who created my inward parts, you knit me together in my mother's womb. I will praise you because I have been remarkably and wondrously made. (Psalm 139:13-14)

---

major news outlets to speak to some of the pressing issues of the day.

But even as they are talking, the ERLC is listening. They are carefully paying attention to broader trends that we may not catch until much later. For example, the ERLC notified congregations about the shifting conversations about gender and sexual ethics in some corners of society in the 1990s—some twenty-five years before this was an issue on the cover of magazines or in the news. They seek to stay on top of things they know will impact our congregations and your personal freedom to express your faith.

RELIGIOUS LIBERTY

The concept of religious liberty seems to always be under attack. Throughout history, governments or other powers have sought to limit and constrain the rights of people to worship how they see fit. In the oppressive environment of the seventeenth century, early Baptists were unable to baptize believers legally. They wrote impassioned treatises asking for liberty. They advocated for the rights of all religions to have the freedom of worship.

In their thinking—and in the thinking of many Baptists today—religious liberty allows for the greatest benefit to all people because it fosters an environment inclined to an open exchange of ideas. In this way, religious liberty contributes to human flourishing. And, an atmosphere of religious liberty allows believers to freely share the greatest news— the gospel!

When everyone has access to the free expression of religious commitment, they are best equipped to live with the positive values of their faith. Churches can worship without government interference. People can speak to issues of the day from the standpoint of Scripture. Even more importantly—every person is seen as having inherent worth.

LIFE

One of the deeply held values of Southern Baptists is our view that every life matters to God. This idea leads Baptists to hold to some basic assumptions about the very essence of life itself.

This is most clearly observed in the ERLC's advocacy against abortion. Based on a clear understanding of Psalm 139, Baptists consistently believe and proclaim that every life has inherent worth, including life in the womb.

Consequently, the ERLC serves on the forefront of this cultural battle by upholding the value of life found in the womb. They sponsor and participate in pro-life rallies, support crisis pregnancy centers in their work, and advocate to end abortion in the halls of Washington D.C. as well as globally.

If life in the womb matters, so do the lives of those already living. The ERLC regularly helps congregations discover ways to minister to individuals with special needs. They also work to aid congregations in preserving the central component of a healthy society—the family. By defending traditional views of marriage on the state and national levels, the goal is to strengthen the God-ordained idea of the family as the primary training ground for children. The family unit, if healthy, sustains societal stability. The ERLC helps families struggling with infertility walk through the complex maze of artificial reproductive technologies and advocate for adoption where appropriate.

In recent years, the ERLC added a focus upon helping individuals and churches think through the challenges of immigration, criminal-justice reform, and human sex trafficking. By connecting with local churches and state conventions, the ERLC continues to lead the way in overcoming these large-scale issues that would be almost impossible for a single congregation to address.

RACIAL RECONCILIATION

One area that the ERLC continues to speak to in our world is the beauty of gospel-centered racial reconciliation. Launching from the teaching of Scripture that humanity is formed in the image of God, the ERLC works tirelessly to think through the complex challenge of race relations.

If all people are "fearfully and wonderfully made" in the image of God, then we can only know God more as we worship together. This understanding of "togetherness" and becoming "one in Christ" changes the dynamics of the local and universal church.

But let's be honest here and take a brief detour.

The SBC started in 1845 with southern churches being unwilling to compromise on their belief about slavery. This is not a great place to begin the conversation about racial reconciliation. Yet God continued to work in the hearts of the people to convict them of their sin of racism. In the 1880s, Baptist churches in the south began to repent of their actions and invest in the education of minority populations.

But old sin-habits die hard. While the ERLC's predecessor in the SBC (the Christian Life Commission) actively sought to bring gospel-centered reconciliation during the Civil Rights Movement of the 1960s, the convention as a whole failed to fully repent of the foundations of our church network.

In 1995, things changed. With their integral work on this particular issue, the ERLC led the way for the convention itself to begin dealing with deep hurt of the past. At the 150th meeting of the Southern Baptist

Convention, the church messengers gathered there stated that the SBC:

- Unwaveringly denounces racism, in all its forms, as deplorable sin;
- Affirms the Bibles teaching that every human life is sacred, and is of equal and immeasurable worth, made in Gods image, regardless of race or ethnicity and needs salvation found only in Christ;
- Laments and repudiates historic acts of evil such as slavery from which we continue to reap a bitter harvest, and recognize that the racism which yet plagues our culture today is inextricably tied to the past;
- Apologizes to all African-Americans for condoning and/or perpetuating individual and systemic racism in our lifetime;
- genuinely repents of racism of which we have been guilty, whether consciously or unconsciously;
- Asks forgiveness from our African-American brothers and sisters, acknowledging that our own healing is at stake;
- Commits ourselves to eradicate racism in all its forms from Southern Baptist life and ministry;
- Commits to pursuing racial reconciliation in all our relationships, especially with our brothers and sisters in Christ for the purpose of the Gospel.[11]

Today, ethnic minority congregations comprise more than 20 percent of all SBC congregations and continue to grow at a rate that is faster than any other denomination. The work on this issue is not yet done, but by God's grace, the SBC is on a trajectory to continually improve the way we reflect the beauty of the gospel through the church as revealed in Ephesians 2:13–16:

> But now in Christ Jesus, you who were far away have been brought near by the blood of Christ. For he is our peace, who made both groups one and tore down the dividing wall of hostility . . . so that he might create in himself one new man from the two, resulting in peace. He did this so that he might reconcile both to God in one body through the cross by which he put the hostility to death.

GETTING LOCAL

"All politics is local," or so the saying goes. Since the ERLC operates on a national and global platform, the important issues at the local level—both in your city or state—aren't overlooked. Local churches are usually quite aware of things happening in their local civic arenas, whether in the local school board or municipality. Congregations can easily work together through their local association or state convention to make a difference in the local community.

State and regional conventions usually connect to the issues happening more broadly at the state level. They often have their own, more regionally focused, commission or network that watches for issues of concern related to religious liberty, family, and life. These commissions work in conjunction with the ERLC to help advocate for the things our congregations are passionate about.

NOT OF THIS WORLD

Jesus reminded his followers, "My kingdom is not of this world" (John 18:36). This idea has important implications. Ultimately, as Christians, we recognize that our true citizenship is in heaven and not here. We don't seek to build kingdoms in this life nor do we pursue political power for power's sake.

The ERLC advocates for Southern Baptists with the intent of helping us maintain freedom of religion and for the sake of the advancement of the Kingdom of God. They are not tied to a specific political party and speak prophetically to anyone who would violate the clear teachings and standards of the Word of God. They do this despite the complexity of many modern issues and concerns, but also do so in love and charity with the hopes of winning many to the Gospel.

As churches, we are not left alone to drown in the overwhelming ocean of culture, but together as a convention, we can accomplish much for the Kingdom of God.

KEY QUESTIONS:

1. What are the main issues that the ERLC helps churches advance?

2. Why is religious liberty so important?

3. Why do issues relating to family and life feature so prominently in the ERLC's work?

4. Visit www.erlc.com/resource-library and discover some of the issues the ERLC is addressing. Commit to praying for one of these issues for the next week.

CHAPTER 7

THE SBC: BETTER TOGETHER

Thirty bullets ripped through the fuselage of his F4 jet. Over 350 miles into North Vietnam, US Air Force pilot Roger Locher was as good as dead when ejected from the cockpit less than forty miles from Hanoi. Landing in a tree, Locker attempted to radio back to base that he had survived. But his voice didn't come through.

The American forces in the south didn't give up on Locher. They monitored the radios. They continued to fly missions into North Vietnam with open coms. For three weeks, Locher wandered the jungles of North Vietnam. Then a flight of F4s flew directly overhead. Locher signaled them. They got word back to the American forces in the south.

General John Vogt of the 7th Air Command was preparing for a raid on Hanoi. Over 150 aircraft including two HH-53C rescue helicopters were preparing to take off. The raid was cancelled upon learning of Locher's plight. Instead, they entire command was sent to rescue Locher.

The result: Locher was rescued without incident because of the overwhelming show of force. When asked why he would dedicate so many resources to rescuing a single man, General Vogt said, "the one thing that keeps our boys motivated is the certain belief that if they go down, we will do absolutely everything we can to get them out."[12] When you are in the military, you are not alone.

So too with Southern Baptists. Churches, pastors, missionaries, evangelists, students, leaders, educators, and church members *are not alone* in their mission. The collective work of the national, state, and local ministries affiliated with the Southern Baptist Convention means we are all in this together. We are better together!

Southern Baptists are not hierarchical. We have no general, no pope, or bishops. No authority structure tells Southern Baptists what to do. Affiliations between Southern Baptists are entirely voluntary. Therefore, *we* are better together as Southern Baptists because *we* commit to each other. We commit to starting churches. We commit to reaching the nations. We commit to engaging the world with the Gospel *together*.

How do we commit to each other? How do we make it so that we are not alone?

Through our missionary work together.

Through our fellowships with one another.

Through our meetings together.

Through each of us taking ownership of every aspect of our collective work.

This chapter explains how you and your church can get involved in the processes and life of the Southern Baptist Convention.

WHY WE CAN'T DO THIS ALONE

In 1 Corinthians 12 Paul mediates a dispute between church members over which spiritual gifts are best. He explains that all the members of a local church need each other. He gives the illustration of the body. Each body part has a different role, a different function.

He then paints an absurd picture. What if the whole body were an eye? It couldn't speak; it couldn't hear; it couldn't touch. Imagine meeting a giant eye ball. It couldn't interact with you; it couldn't shake your hand; and it couldn't talk to you. If something

---

Become a Messenger

Every Southern Baptist church that contributes to SBC causes can send at least two messengers to the annual meeting of the SBC. The more your church gives (either as a percentage of its total giving or as total dollar amount), the more messengers it can send. Your church chooses whom it sends. Those it chooses can register for the meeting at www.sbcannualmeeting.net.

Get involved, sign up, and show up to be more involved in the process for reaching the world with the gospel.

---

got caught in its eye, it couldn't do anything about it. It would be completely inadequate to do all that a body can do because it was just an eye. The body needs all its parts to function properly.

Paul's analogy obviously is meant to apply in the life of the local church. Each church needs different types of people to function within and reach its community.

Paul's analogy also applies to churches working together. Like church members, SBC churches are different. Black, white, rich, poor, old, young, diverse, contemporary, traditional, reformed, revivalist, small, urban, rural—you get the idea. To reach our nation and our world with the gospel, we need each other.

Just as the body needs each part, Southern Baptists need each of us. In previous chapters we have outlined some practical ways for you to get involved in SBC ministries. In this chapter we want to demonstrate how each of us can functions within this convention and how the work of the Southern Baptist needs every one of us.

MEETINGS, TRUSTEES, AND COMMITTEES: A PROCESS THAT INVITES EVERYONE

Your association, state convention, and the national SBC each has developed a process for involving every type of Southern Baptist in its governance. This process begins with the annual meeting where we discuss our collective work and how we can best utilize our collective strengths to reach the nations.

Southern Baptists work together voluntarily. We don't have a hierarchy. We do this because we believe that every Christian stands accountable to God for his actions and ministry:

- That every soul is competent to respond to the Lordship of Christ.
- That collectively each church member is a priest before God.
- That each church stands autonomously before God for its ministry.

As a result, no church has spiritual authority over any other. The ministries we have exist because we all agree to create them. We all agree to fund them. We all agree that we need them.

This means that churches and their members oversee the ministries of the Southern Baptist Convention. The ministries this book has been about *do not exist* apart from the churches. They *do not exist* apart from you. The ministries of the Convention are *your* church's ministries.

Because we own our work together, a meeting where every Southern Baptist church can send messengers to speak up and to vote is the way by which Southern Baptists direct their ministries. It is the primary way you and your church commit to furthering our work together.

These meetings *are* the convention. Other denominations are built around hierarchies and exist all the time. Not the SBC. While our work continues and is tangibly present, our convention is not. We have an annual meeting to which every church sends messengers to have a voice and a vote on the ministry activities for the next year, and then the convention "disappears" as the ministries carry forward. Your church can and should send messengers to the Convention because it's yours.

THE ANNUAL MEETINGS: WHAT HAPPENS?

The Southern Baptist Convention ensures that no entity, no pastor, no church, is alone in making disciples. The annual meeting makes this happens as:

1. We discuss and vote on budgets. When we do, we make sure that what we support advances the gospel.
2. We elect, hear from, and even ask questions of leaders. When we do, we see how the collective work of the Convention comes alongside our individual work to make a larger gospel difference.
3. We hear reports from missionaries on the field. When we do, we see how we together are changing our world as people come to faith in Christ.
4. We speak to the issues of our culture through resolutions and motions. When we do, we

clarify to a watching world how the Bible speaks to current issues.

5. We rally around our common Biblical commitments. When we do, we safeguard the faith once for all delivered to the saints for the next generation.[13]

6. We talk with and fellowship with one another. When we do, we make each other aware of our various needs so that we can develop new initiatives to support each other.

7. We pray with, hear sermons from, and sing praises to God with one another. When we do, we our brought together under the Lordship of our common Savior.

In short, through business meetings, we demonstrate how we are better together.

TRUSTEES AND THE EXECUTIVE COMMITTEE: OTHER ASPECTS OF OUR PROCESS

While the Southern Baptist Convention sets the trajectory for all the ministries of the convention, Southern Baptists appoint trustees and an executive committee to oversee the day-to-day operation of the various ministries.

Trustees. Every year the Southern Baptists Convention elects a president who moderates the annual meetings, promotes the work of the convention, and begins the process of nominating trustees which are

The Bible:
What Holds Southern Baptists Together

In 1999, messengers to the Southern Baptist Convention requested that a committee update the Baptist Faith and Message. At the 2000 Annual Meeting the committee made its recommendation. The committee had tightened the language regarding the Bible.

Over the previous few decades a small but vocal group had inserted itself in SBC life. They argued that the Bible contained errors. The committee wanted to make it clear that Southern Baptists believe the Bible is fully inspired and without error. Anthony Sizemore, a Texas pastor, objected to the language and proposed a return to the earlier, less precise language. He explained that while the Bible is "true and trustworthy . . . It is ultimately just a book."

There was an audible gasp in the room. Al Mohler responded in favor of the language the committee recommended. This was the issue that would define who Southern Baptists were, he argued.

A period of debate followed. Was the Bible just a book or was it the Word of God?

The decision. The return to the less precise language was soundly defeated. Nearly 95 percent of the tens of thousands of people gathered stood to affirm the committee's report. Southern Baptists made it clear. The Bible is the foundation for all that we do, all that we believe.

later voted upon by the convention to serve for a specified term. The trustees are volunteers. They are pastors and laypersons. They come from all around the country. The convention empowers trustees to oversee the day-to-day governance of each ministry.

The Executive Committee. The Southern Baptist Convention meets for two days a year. During the rest of the year, Southern Baptist interests are represented by members of the executive committee, who are chosen from churches from all over the country. This committee selects a president who oversees the day-to-day operations of the Convention. The executive committee explains the work of the Convention and its ministries to both Southern Baptists and the larger world through Baptist Press (www.bpnews.net). It also manages the business of the Convention, arranges the annual meeting, offers advice on how various ministries can work together, and oversees the distribution of the Cooperative Program. It is incredibly efficient in all of these tasks. While most non-profits dedicate a sizable portion of their revenue to such task, the executive committee uses about 1 percent of Cooperative Program revenues for these tasks.

STATE CONVENTIONS AND ASSOCIATIONAL MEETINGS

Just as the processes of the Southern Baptist Convention provide a means by which we all have ownership of its ministries, so do the state conventions and local associations. Through their respective meetings, committees, and trustees, we all are invited to take ownership of the ministries of our state conventions and associations. Get involved in these meetings. As you do, you'll learn how to pray for various ministries. You'll gain a greater awareness of all that your Cooperative Program giving does. You'll

Guidestone and Mission:Dignity
Portions from John Ambra

Those who serve Southern Baptist are cared for by Southern Baptists. Historically, Baptists have not been a wealthy people. As a result, many Baptist ministers, missionaries, and denominational employees do not have much money. Many churches struggle to provide adequate benefits for their pastors. This is where Guidestone Resources comes in. It provides an array of affordable retirement and life insurance options to help churches take care of their pastors. It even offers a program called Mission:Dignity for those pastors and their widows who enter the retirement years with little. Guidestone is another example of how Southern Baptists are better together.

Idell Austin went to bed hungry because money was in short supply. She has been helped through Mission:Dignity. Her husband Wayne pastored small churches in North Carolina for almost forty years. When he died, there was no burial insurance and hospital bills piled up. Idell had to work in a local textile mill until she was 73 years old just to pay off the bills. When she retired, her $700-a-month Social Security check was all she had. "When you draw $700 a month, you pay your light bill, telephone, taxes on your car, gas, and medicine. There's nothing left," she said.

A local pastor heard about her plight and suggested she seek assistance from GuideStone. She is grateful to those who help her live in dignity and security. "I was going to bed quite a few times eating only a slice of bread and drinking a glass of water," she said. "And I have gone to bed hungry because I want my bills paid, and I have to pay for my medicine."

Speaking of all those who support the ministry, she says one thing: "Lord bless them! I got something to eat tonight- and it wasn't just a piece of toast."

Almost daily, thank-you cards arrive from Mission:Dignity recipients who tell how the monthly support makes the difference between having food or medicine, or doing without.

If you would like to join with others in caring for these precious men and women—or if you or someone you know might be blessed receiving assistance—please contact Mission:Dignity http://www.missiondignity.org/.

be encouraged by the stories of lives changed. You'll discover new ways to share your faith and new ministries through which you can volunteer and serve others. Through the processes of our conventions, we work together to advance the Great Commission and change a lost world.

THE COOPERATIVE PROGRAM: HOW WE SUPPORT OUR WORK

The Annual Meetings, Executive Committee, and trustee system are the processes by which all Southern Baptists inform what cooperative ministries look like. The Cooperative Program (CP) is the process we use to support these ministries. It funds all that Southern Baptist do. When you and your church send a check to your state convention, you are funding the Cooperative Program.

Through CP you support children's homes, disaster relief, and other ministries in your state.

Through CP you fund the education of Baptist college and seminary students.

Through CP, you fund missionaries across North America and around the world.

Through CP, we collectively engage our culture.

When you and your church give through the CP, you make a difference, you change the world.

AN INVITATION TO JOIN US

Southern Baptists will not rest until the entire world knows about Jesus. This happens as we go and tell. This happens as we serve. This happens as we teach. This happens as we engage our culture and our world.

We want to make a difference. We want to see the gospel change our cities, our states, our regions, our nation, and all other nations. Through the Cooperative Program, through service in our local churches, through partnerships with each other, and even through our business meetings, you and your church make that difference.

You push back lostness through our gospel partnership. You minister to the least of these through ministries to those in need. You train the next generation through our educational ministries. You are changing the world.

God uses Southern Baptists to change the world. Our unique structures and processes ensure scriptural faithfulness and the priority of reaching the lost for Christ. While none of us can change the world on our own, when you are a Southern Baptist, you are not alone. *Together* we fulfill the Great Commission and we reach the world because of the gospel. And we are better together!

KEY QUESTIONS

1. Read 1 Corinthians 12:12–27. Why do churches need different types of people? What are some of the advantages of different types of churches working together?

2. Take a look at the website of the SBC Annual Meeting here: http://www.sbcannualmeeting.net/sbc18/. Have you ever attended one of these meetings? If so what was it like? If not, what do you think would be the result of you attending an Annual Meeting of the SBC?

3. Southern Baptist share a series of doctrinal commitments expressed in the Baptist Faith and Message 2000. The BFM 2000 can be found here: http://www.sbc.net/bfm2000/bfm2000.asp. Read the first article on the Scriptures. Why do you think it's important that churches agree on what the Bible is to cooperate with one another?

4. After reading this book, what are some reasons you see for supporting the Cooperative Program? How will you encourage your church to become more involved in the SBC and in giving to support SBC ministries?

AUTHOR BIOS

Robert J. Matz (PhD Liberty University) is Assistant Professor of Christian studies at Midwestern Baptist Theological Seminary and pastors a local SBC church. He teaches in a wide variety of subject matters and is passionate about helping Christians follow Christ. He and his wife Jessica reside in Kansas City, MO and have three children.

John Mark Yeats (PhD Trinity Evangelical Divinity School) is the Dean of Students at Midwestern Baptist Theological Seminary and Associate Professor of Church History. He enjoys helping congregations connect to the joy they can have working together for the sake of the gospel. He and his wife, Angie, live in Kansas City, MO, and have four children.

ENDNOTES

1. All Biblical citations are taken from the Christian Standard Bible (Nashville: Holman Bible Publishers, 2017).
2. See also the repetition of this picture in I Cor 11:3; Eph 1:22; 5:23; and Col 2:10.
3. Dan Kimball, *They Love Jesus but Not the Church* (Grand Rapids: Zondervan, 2009).
4. Paul Chitwood and John L. Yeats, "The Future of Baptist State Conventions," in *The SBC and the 21st Century*, ed. Jason Allen (Nashville: Broadman and Holman, 2016), 57.
5. The proceedings of the 1846 meeting of the Southern Baptist Convention, 17.
6. Tammy's Story and more like it are found at https://www.sendrelief.org/news/survival-stories-human-trafficking/. Reproduced with permission from the North American Mission Board.
7. SBC Constitution
8. Bob Smietana, "The Southern Baptist Spending Crunch: The missions agency of the largest US Protestant denomination faces a $21 million deficit. Could it spell the end of the full-time

missionary?" Christianity Today 59, no. 9 (November 2015): 64.

9. IMB Mission and Vision Statement https://www.imb.org/vision-and-mission/

10. For more on this trip see Jenny Gregory, "TMC Students Share the Gospel in El Salvador; 627 Saved," *Truett-McConnell University*, June 23, 2015, https://truett.edu/news/archive/tmc-students-share-the-gospel-in-el-salvador-627-saved/.

11. To see the full resolution, visit http://www.sbc.net/resolutions/899/resolution-on-racial-reconciliation-on-the-150th-anniversary-of-the-southern-baptist-convention.

12. Kevin O'Rourke, *Taking Fire: Saving Captain Aikman: A Story of the Vietnam Air War*, (New York: Casemate, 2013) 110.

13. See http://www.bpnews.net/6063.

Made in the USA
Coppell, TX
28 May 2020

26597126R00080